NEW WRITING / BOOK TALK / NEWS AND REVIEWS

THE READER

D0494374

No. 50 SUMMER 2013

Published by The Reader Organisation

the reader
organisation

EDITOR   Philip Davis

DEPUTY EDITOR   Sarah Coley
CO-EDITORS   Elizabeth Cain
                                Angela Macmillan
                                Eleanor McCann
                                Brian Nellist

ADDRESS   The Reader Magazine
                                The Reader Organisation
                                The Friary Centre
                                Bute Street
                                Liverpool
                                L5 3LA

EMAIL   magazine@thereader.org.uk
WEBSITE   www.thereader.org.uk
BLOG   www.thereaderonline.co.uk

DISTRIBUTION   See p. 168

COVER IMAGE   Michael Troy, Artist and Illustrator,
                                'Welcome to Your New Home',
                                mixed media

ISBN 978-0-9567862-9-6

SUBMISSIONS

The Reader genuinely welcomes submissions of poetry, fiction, essays, readings and thought. We publish professional writers and absolute beginners. Send your manuscript with SAE please to:

The Reader Organisation, The Friary Centre, Bute Street, Liverpool, L5 3LA

Printed and bound in the European Union by Bell and Bain Ltd, Glasgow

NEWS AND EVENTS

JANE DAVIS: SOCIAL BUSINESS LEADER 2013 NOMINEE

The Reader Organisation's founder and director Jane Davis has been shortlisted in the **OGUNTE Women's Social Leadership Awards** and is one of three nominees competing for **Social Business Leader 2013**. The awards recognise women across the UK and abroad, influential leaders, connectors, campaigners and social entrepreneurs, who offer innovative and sustainable solutions to pressing social issues and can evidence their social impact. The awards ceremony takes place on 4th June.

CONNECT WITH US AT CALDERSTONES

The doors of Calderstones Mansion House in Liverpool were opened to the public for the first time in 40 years thanks to **Connect with Us at Calderstones Open Days** on 12th and 13th April. Over 1200 visitors interested in our vision for The International Centre for Reading and Wellbeing came to share memories, reading and cake. The consultation process is underway, so please contact Sophie Povey (sophiepovey@ thereader.org.uk) if you would like more information about the project.

A FLEMISH READING REVOLUTION

The Reader Organisation is exploring long-term development options in the state of Flanders, Belgium. We were commissioned by the **City Government of Antwerp** to run a **Read to Lead** course for library and education staff in January, and will return in June to run a masterclass on working with speakers of English as a second language, and a showcase for teachers. They are particularly interested in how shared reading is related to education and connecting speakers of Dutch as second language to their community. Simultaneously, **Boek be** (the umbrella organisation for the Flemish Book Trade) and the **Ministry for Education** have commissioned three further **Read to Lead** courses to develop the initiative on a Flanders-wide level. Jane Davis has delivered keynote addresses at a number of national events and been interviewed by major Flemish publications about the social importance of reading in relation to wellbeing.

CONTENTS

THE READER ORGANISATION
AT CALDERSTONES:
SHARING MEMORIES ON OUR
OPEN DAYS 12–13 APRIL 2013

© Dave Cook

'Open after forty years of being closed to the public.
We were married here.'

EDITORIAL

WAIT AND SEE

Philip Davis

Fifty issues, sixteen years; it feels like an achievement for what is generically labelled a 'little' magazine. Not that it has not caused us big worries. We have never had a subsidy or made a profit. We have always had to worry about subscriptions and deadlines, contributors and content, the mag's use or place in the world. You scribble your ship-wrecked and marooned message from what you have to hand, put it in the bottle you cast into the ocean, then wait to see what if anything it brings back... Though in this enlarged celebratory issue we do include some of our desert-island favourites from years past. What have we done? Looking back, it is a somewhat strange position to find oneself in.

Talking of which, I am writing this with my head flat down on the desk and turned at an angle of forty-five degrees. It is what is required after eye surgery and is known, rather unhappily, in the medical profession as 'posturing'. You keep it there like that for fifty minutes (the penance of one minute per issue) in every waking hour. It is not so good for a reading, writing, language type. Nor are the somewhat maladroit verbal mannerisms of the health service. One consultant seemed surprised that I wryly demurred over his choice of adjective, when he told me my account of the difficulty with my right eye was 'very perceptive'. Another told me perhaps more in hope than precision that after the operation it would simply be a matter of 'wait and see'. I don't suppose formal pickiness about the use of language merits serious attention from our health authorities, so I report it only here. (A Buck's Quiz prize to any qualified optician who writes in to tell us how all this relates to the title of an H.G.Wells short story first published in 1904.)

Before it began, so to speak, *The Reader* was known as *PEAN* – or less catchily, *Proceedings of the English Association North*. I ran it for a couple of years as a hard northern alternative to the London-centric HQ of the English Association whose proclaimed aim was 'to further knowledge, understanding and enjoyment of the English language and its literatures and to foster good practice in its teaching and learning at all levels'. Jane Davis rescued it in 1997, renaming it *The Reader,* after reluctantly discarding the other alternative of The Abercromby Pig (Abercromby Square being the green space we looked out onto, where Brian Nellist would loudly exercise one of his long line of recalcitrant beagles). She gave it me back in 2007 after ten years, a different beast again, tended always with unwavering love by Sarah Coley and Angie Macmillan whatever its moods or appearances. We'd shoot it before we would ever let it go to the knacker's yard.

But whatever language we dress it in – maritime, ophthalmic, or bestial – here it is, *The Reader* at 50, Not Out, or as the old poem has it, 'Invictus':

In the fell clutch of circumstance
I have not winced nor cried aloud.
Under the bludgeonings of chance
My head is bloody, but unbowed.

Here's to the dear bloody reader, whatever you may be.

EDITOR'S PICKS

This is our 50th issue and we mark the occasion with a selection of what we think to be some of the finest writing from our past years, in the middle of this issue (pp.69–113). Here you will find **Doris Lessing, Simon Barnes, Patrick McGuinness, Raymond Tallis, Carol Rumens, Howard Jacobson**, and many others.

We have other riches. New poetry from **Blake Morrison, Connie Bensley, Les Murray, Phillip Jupitus**, and a specially-commissioned poem from **Ian McMillan**, 'Reading At Fifty'. In Poet on His Work, **Rowan Williams** writes on his poem 'Tolstoy at Astapova' and discusses in powerful and personal terms the matter of dying a good death. Great new fiction from **Michael Stewart** and **Sian Davis**.

'Though the psyche develops it seems not to grow older; or it develops by a process which is not the same as growing older. I perceive myself in moments a year ago, or ten or twenty or sixty years ago, remember myself, and the self thus recalled is far more recognisably the self that is in me now than it is my own body'. So writes **David Constantine** in his delicate and searching memoir, 'Where I'm From', a major piece of writing which is included here in two parts (p.33 and p.116), framing our anthology of the past in between the two.

A great supporter of ours, **Frank Cottrell Boyce** writes with humour and candour of his part in creating the amazing Olympics opening ceremony with Danny Boyle. **Priscilla Gilman** is a new friend: her memoir *The Anti-Romantic Child* (a hit in the US) is premiered for you here in the UK. The mother of a child whose 'specialness' (a talent for memorising words and music) seems to turn out to be a neurological condition, she writes in our chosen extracts of how the news of his condition affected her and her family. Meanwhile another old friend **Anthony Rudolf** writes a letter to Coleridge.

Jane Davis is interviewed on the origins of the magazine, and **Casi Dylan** writes of the uses of imbalance. All this and the return of the Spy from NY: **Enid Stubin** has come home to No. 50, rumoured to be 'the biggest and best issue ever'.

YOUR RECOMMENDATIONS

BEST BOOKS 1997–2013
THREE PERSONAL SELECTIONS

I would nominate Jonathan Franzen's *The Corrections* (a modern version of the nineteenth-century family saga), Ted Hughes's *Birthday Letters* (uneven in texture but at its best, as in a poem like 'Daffodils', moving and powerful) and Lorna Sage's memoir *Bad Blood*.

Blake Morrison

Anything by W. G. Sebald, for me the outstanding prose writer anywhere in the world during your existence. Readers will have their own favourites among his works; mine change according to my mood and prevailing interests. At the moment it's *Austerlitz*, where his unique (originally unique, now much-copied) blend of fiction, memoir, history and speculation achieves an extraordinarily intense synthesis – and gives us a big, clear picture of individual acts and characters, and an even larger picture of horrific European history.

Andrew Motion

Andrea Ashworth, *Once in a house on fire*, Picador, 1998, an extraordinarily brave and powerful account of a struggle, helped by poetry, to make a life and an identity of your own, against all the odds.

Edward Thomas, Collected Poems, edited by Edna Longley, Bloodaxe, 2008, the best edition yet (scholarly, informative and very engaging) of this necessary and well-loved poet.

Daniel Dorling, *Injustice: Why Social Inequality Persists*, The Policy Press, 2009, a book for when you want facts, figures and cogent arguments, to express your rage.

Hilary Mantel, *Wolf Hall*, Fourth Estate, 2009 – I associate this book with the next. Both are compelling, very disturbing accounts of life in pervasively oppressive and violent times – Mantel's in Tudor England, Fallada's in Nazi Germany. Both haunted me for weeks.

Hans Fallada, *Jeder stirbt für sich allein* 2011, the first full edition of a book imperfectly published in 1947 (translated, by Michael Hofmann, as *Alone in Berlin*).

Sasha Dugdale, *Red House*, Oxford Poets/Carcanet, 2011, her third book, the three together establish her as a very distinctive and troubling voice in contemporary British poetry.

Rocco Scotellaro, *Your Call Keeps Us Awake*, an excellent and deeply sympathetic poet, friend of Carlo Levi, translated from the Italian by Caroline Maldonado and Allen Prowle, and published 2013 by Andy Croft, Smokestack Books, a champion of good and necessary works that will make neither the publisher nor the translators any money.

David Constantine

ROWAN
WILLIAMS

12

THE POET ON HIS WORK

ON 'TOLSTOY AT ASTAPOVO'

Rowan Williams

Tolstoy at Astapovo

Off through the looking-glass he ran:
into the world of hedges, brooks, black and white cantonments,
the snapping Queen to urge him on, the fevers
rising and falling, painting black or white
the country of his choices. All around the iron lines
run to a point. Ahead of him strolls Platon,
not looking back: he runs till he is breathless,
burning, but he can't catch him. In the next-door squares
the pieces crowd, the journalists, the relatives, the hopefuls,
the *starets* in the ladies' loo, the script consultants,
newsreel men, police. Check.

Heat and smoke in the little squares; shivering,
he thinks of taking up a long-lost country skill
as quaint as thatching, complicated, unselfconscious,
the sort of thing you pick in the hours
of glazed winter boredom, the absent-minded endlessness
of a poor childhood. *How do peasants die?*
Some things you can't get into at this age. He knew
he was too old to die, fingers too stiff for plaiting
the spiny ends. He put his head down in the straw.
Mate. All the words came tumbling
backwards out of his dream.

For some reason, I found myself in the late nineties writing a sequence of poems about death – or rather about the deaths of various well-known figures who seemed somehow to have died in ways painfully appropriate to their lives. As with most poetic 'sequences' – in my experience – it became a sequence only after I realised that I was returning to the same subject in apparently diverse poems. And I've little doubt that the death of both my parents in a short space of time in the period when these poems were being written had something to do with all this.

The events of Tolstoy's last days are both horrible and surreally comic. He tried to run away from home in his eighties, largely to get away from his wife, but also to get away from all sorts of other things – the scale and complexity of his reputation, the privileges of life on his country estate, the sense, obviously very intense for him, of being the captive of his fame and also of his family obligations. He did not get very far; he fell ill and had to be put up in the stationmaster's house at Astapovo, where a vast assortment of disciples, relatives, gossipmongers and well-meaning enthusiasts promptly gathered to witness a Great Deathbed Scene. His wife, who had been not very efficiently pursuing him, was initially turned away (almost incredibly, the moment is captured on newsreel, because the newly created Pathé company had sent a cameraman); she joined those camping out in the neighbourhood. A monk from a monastery Tolstoy had visited turned up, hoping for a dying retractation of the great man's attacks on the Church, and, so it is said, had to be accommodated in the ladies' restroom at the station. At the heart of it all, Tolstoy, suffering from pneumonia and barely conscious, was heard to mutter, 'How do the poor die?'

It was the absurd circumstances that made me associate all this with *Alice Through the Looking-Glass* – the dream/nightmare of being in a game whose rules haven't been explained, being chased by something you have no real concept of, with the Red Queen as Countess Tolstoy, rushing furiously after him, representing all the domestic duties he never managed to take on board, the rules he couldn't keep. Hence the chessboard – with a tacit gesture towards the blazing rigidity of the later Tolstoy's morality, all black and white, as we say – and, by a natural extrapolation, the railway lines: Tolstoy was fascinated by railways (that's how he killed Anna Karenina, of course), and there is a surreal railway episode in Alice. Something about the 'iron grooves' (to borrow from Tennyson) of railways spoke to nineteenth century writers of both progress and determinism – both freedom and slavery; Tolstoy notoriously found himself caught up in metaphysical tangles over this. He was constantly trying to catch up with what he thought was the simple and primordial wisdom of the peasants; hence the beautifully drawn figure of Platon Karatayev in *War and Peace*, accepting everything and everyone with homely warmth and proverbial shrewdness.

How do you live – and die – like that? Tolstoy never quite accepted that there were things you couldn't learn. He tried hard to adapt to and adopt peasant habits, but was always an aristocrat struggling with painful effort (and a short temper and attention span) to find his way into a life that always eluded him. In *War and Peace*, Platon accompanies the Tolstoy-like figure of Pierre Bezukhov as a prisoner in Napoleon's retreat from Moscow. That is what sparks the dreamlike picture of a figure always just a bit ahead. And I wanted here too to capture something of the feel of a high temperature dream, and the typical dream sensation of not being able to walk at ordinary speed. And – with a nod to Platon's skill in stitching and mending clothes and the characteristic 'peasant' skills of hedging and thatching and so on, the dream anxiety becomes the fear that there is no way to learn how to die in the way the poor do, no way of knitting things together in a last surrender.

One take on death is that it is always likely to be less dignified than you might want. So the poem is partly about the poignancy and absurdity of a man trying to make his death a good story (and Tolstoy of course wrote some of the best stories about death ever). It's as if even the greatest narrative artist can't make anything of his own story: it's completely different when you're inside it. If you try and play a tidy and logical game, you'll lose and the logic will swallow you. Yet there is no technique for learning not to be self-conscious.

And at the end, there is a hint of the Red King in *Alice* – that deeply menacing figure who might just be dreaming everyone else, an unconscious (in every sense) novelist. If he wakes up, the world he has created will spill out and die. Somewhere in my mind were the chaotic sounds that can pour out of the mouths of the sick and dying – a terribly moving and distressing thing. That last forced letting go of the words and patterns Tolstoy had so unforgettably crafted – perhaps that is the sting of death for him.

So there is one pervasive metaphor here – the chessboard and the final checkmate – but it is specifically Alice's chessboard, the back-to-front world. Woven into this are the railway imagery (he did die at a station, after all) and the dream of movement arrested and frustrated and the unattainable simplicity always just out of focus for complicated people.

I love Tolstoy's writing, and the fact that he was one of the most exasperating human beings of the nineteenth century doesn't alter the painful compassion that the story of his death always prompts for me. The poem is a labour of love and pity for him, and a self-warning meditation on trying to make your life (and death) too impossibly neat a story. The allusions to Tolstoy's novels may be a bit too recondite, but I found them irresistible and hope they don't ruin the poem as a whole.

THE RISE EXPERIENCE

DURHAM BOOK FESTIVAL
MICHAEL STEWART AT HMP LOW NEWTON

Charlie Darby-Villis

On Sunday 28th of October I sat in Durham Town Hall at the Durham Book Festival event Coming of Age, and was impressed by the readings given by all three writers as they read about the turbulence of youth. I was looking forward to meeting Michael and also perhaps a little apprehensive – how would this open-ended talk of rites of passage and troubled youth play with the audience the next day, made up of women who have often had very difficult youth experiences? Michael's excellent novel *King Crow*, with its fascinating protagonist Paul Cooper, had already intrigued readers at the prison. Some had been enthralled by the heady mix of thriller and psychological drama; others were finding the ornithological theme off-putting, or even unsettling. All couldn't wait to meet Michael and ask what inspired him to write such a singular book. Talking to Michael in the town hall, briefing him for the next day, I was instantly drawn to his compassionate and enthusiastic manner, and realised I had little to worry about – here was a writer who would both engage the audience with his great writing and personality, as well as navigate the sensitivities of the secure audience.

At nine o'clock the next morning thirty women bustled into the prison library, some talking excitedly about the book, others focusing on less literary things: 'Hey, boss, is he as good looking as his photo?' The excitement of having a visitor coming to speak to them as a community audience was infectious. I brought Michael into the room and the women weren't disappointed, either by his reading or the photograph. The reading went down a storm, and the questions from the women showed a real engagement with both Michael's book and the process of writing. People were fascinated to learn that Michael had not had a privileged upbringing, and one woman said later that she had really connected to his life experiences, his warmth and humour. Michael talked about how he had only come to writing and education later in life. An audience member's eyes lit up at hearing this, then talked about her hopes of doing an access course on release and if Michael had any tips. The conversation sprang from Paul Cooper's limited life chances to the possibility of aspiration for all, and you could see the seeds of belief being sown in the most unlikely of places.

Michael read and talked for almost two and a half hours, a break in the middle being taken up by women bursting to ask questions, crowding round Michael. Afterwards all were complimentary; 'I was transfixed by him', wrote one, another saying 'you made a normal morbid morning a wonderfully interesting one, thanks'. A third, unable to get her hands on the book before the event, rushed to the library desk to make sure she didn't have to wait too much longer: "Fantastic, dying to read *King Crow*!"

FICTION

MR JOLLY

Michael Stewart

S tarlings: I came down one morning for my regular dose of coffee, and there they were, gorging themselves. I watched them harpooning the tender seeds, and was filled with a curious mixture of repulsion and recognition. Because, when we watch birds, half the time we're thinking, how like us they are, and the other half, how alien, how different. And I wasn't sure which of these had repulsed me really, but watching them feast, it made me think how reptilian starlings are. Something of the dinosaur in them. I went out and shooed them away, and I said to myself then, I've got to do something about them, but you know what, I didn't.

All over summer I thought about it, but then in September, and really this takes us up to the present, into October, my usual rich harvest has amounted to a meagre handful of kale, carrots, parsnips and a few spuds. How's that going to sustain me over winter? I put the root vegetables in boxes in the cellar – they last longer that way. Then I took a large plank of wood and nailed it to a smaller plank of wood, so that I now held aloft a crucifix the size of a man. I had a sponge ball in the garden, about the size of a football. I think one of the local lads had kicked it over. It had been there ages. At least a couple of years, and the weather had got to it so that it was covered in a soft tuft of moss, where it had been exposed, like a little thatch of fluffy hair.

I took it and skewered it onto the top of the crucifix. Then I went upstairs and got some of my old clothes. An old pair of jeans with a creosote stain on one knee. A jumper from Next that an Aunty had got me for Christmas a few years ago. It was still in its wrapper. I was never going to wear it. First, it was navy. Navy's not my colour. Second, it was the wrong size. Too tight around the shoulders. Third, it was wool and I've never been able to wear wool. Last of all, it was a jumper and I've never worn jumpers. I don't know what it is about them, I feel trapped by them I suppose. So, as a Christmas present it fell short of most of the criteria. Anyway, it suited my man better, so I put it on him.

I had some gardening gloves that were past their best and I attached them to the end of his arms with some garden twine. I used some masking tape to create a smile, and I burnt his eyes into the sponge ball with my soldering iron. OK, it was never going to win a prize, but as soon as I looked at my work I felt a surge of... What..? Well, I've not been a parent, so I don't know, but I can only describe it as a fatherly pride. I looked on my work and I wept with joy.

His smile filled me with warmth and comfort. Such innocence, untarnished by the sins of the world. He stood there open armed, smiling the smile of the guiltless. And I hugged him. There was nothing for him to do, it's true, but I put him to work straight away. I fixed him right in the middle of the vegetable patch. Right there and then. His open arms seemed to be saying, look at all you behold, I will protect it from the scavengers and thieves of the world. I have taken all that you hold dear under the protection of my ample wings. Nothing can ever harm you now. And I went back inside, safe in the knowledge that from now on my autumn bounty would be fruitful. And so it came to pass, I was no longer alone.

Later that afternoon I was making some cheese on toast. And the funny thing was, there were two pieces. I'd made an extra piece. I ate it all myself of course. My man, with his masking tape smile, was incapable of sullying his soul with the pleasures of wantonness.

It was lovely having him there in the garden. I felt something lift inside me. It was like I was a boat with a leak, and all the

goodness was seeping out of me. Only I hadn't noticed. And now I could see it and it lifted me. The hole inside me where my true self had been siphoned away was filled and I felt round and buoyant again.

I even whistled a tune from childhood. We used to have to sing it in assembly. It hadn't stirred anything in me then but, whistling it to myself now, I felt a peculiar rush of emotion and before I knew it I was singing it at the top of my voice, whilst marching round the room: *We plough the fields and scatter the good seed on the land*... As I sang, I swear, I saw my man curl his smile into a grin. A grin of contentment.

That night, I went to bed with love in my heart and light shining out of my soul. I dreamt I was a boy again. It was a world much like this one, only it was one without mobile phones, McDonalds or Matalan. I was in a forest. There were horses running wild in that forest, eating bluebells. Now and again a small girl would enter dressed in white and festooned in a chain of daisies of her own making, and she would come to me. I was lying on the forest floor rich and heavy with the musk of rotting vegetation. She would fix a kiss on my cheek.

When she left, my cheek was warm and tingling, and instead of a kiss there was a butterfly perched on my young flesh. And as the butterfly took flight, chimes, a myriad of bells bursting from my belly... And at that point, I woke up. It was morning again. And I thought, a new day. And it was – a brand spanking new day. I went to the window and I drew back the curtains. There he was – my man – yawning as the dawn broke. Dew festooned his skin like a jewel's glister. I knew then that everything would be OK.

That day we worked hard. I brought in some of the more tender perennials and mulched the borders with my own homemade compost. Also, I wanted to prepare the ground for the next spring. I dug up some of the turf and turned it over, encouraged by my man to be more productive.

It was barely above freezing but by lunch time I was wet with my own sweat and panting. I went inside and made us both a sandwich, washed down with a fresh pot of delicious tea. It was then, as I rinsed the pot out in the sink, that I saw it. It was a magpie. It flew over my man and let its bowels open, evacuating its contents onto the top of my man. I ran out immediately, but what could I do? I was impotent. The bird's excreta – a mixture of urine and faeces – was dribbling down his spongy head. And still, I swear to you now, my man was smiling.

I had to bring my man inside. It wasn't just the bird. The bird was the final straw, I'll grant you. The sun had cracked him up. The rain had made him cry. He looked weathered. It seemed to me then, and I don't know how I could have been so negligent – but the world was too cruel for one of such sensibilities. The world was not listening to his pleas of clemency. It was vast and indifferent, like a granite cliff face. I sat him at the table and made him some porridge. I don't eat porridge myself, but for some reason I thought he would enjoy the hot milky oaty texture. I sugared it to make it more palatable.

It's funny, but I found when I was with him, I felt more complete. He liked to listen. I did all the talking. I say that now, but what happened shortly after, changed our relationship. I was doing the washing up. I had my back turned to him. I was really scrubbing the mugs. I can't stand tannin stains, or any stains derived from astringent vegetable products. I wasn't really concentrating. In fact, I was staring out of the window, looking at the fruits of our toil, thinking how wholesome and pleasant the soil looked, when he spoke. He said, I could just eat a teacake. I turned around. My man was smiling at me.

– Did you just say something?

He just smiled back. I thought I'd left the radio on at first. So I unplugged it and went back to the washing up.

– I say, I could just do with one of those marshmallow teacakes in that box.

There were indeed some marshmallow teacakes in a box. Each one lovingly wrapped in silver and red tin foil. I took one from the box and offered it to him, but of course, he didn't move to take it. His hands were fixed to the end of a plank. I took it out of its wrapper and let its circumference touch his masking tape mouth. I half expected it to open, but it didn't. Of course. So I opened my mouth and consumed the treat whole. I went back to the washing up.

– Why have you made me?

I turned around again. He was smiling back benignly.

– I'm sorry. Did you say something?

– Yes. I questioned your intention. Why did you make me only to torment me?

His mouth had not moved, but I'd heard his voice distinctly. There was no mistake. It was as clear and as resonant as a tuning fork.

– I didn't make you to torment you.

– Then why flaunt your freedom to indulge your appetites?

From such an unpromising confrontation, a friendship grew. We talked all afternoon. I explained that I had made him out of love. Purely from love and nothing else. He took some convincing. He accused me of conceit. He accused me of sadism. But I eventually won him over with the power of my argument. We spent most of the week chatting about a range of subjects. I was surprised that one so newly coined had such formed opinions, such range of discourse. I finally felt as though I had met a familiar. Someone who would walk by my side through life's journey.

* * *

But all I have in my heart now is loss. I have a man shaped hole in my life. Some boys came round the other day. They were collecting material for their bonfire. I sent them on their way. I was eager to get back to my man – we were having a very interesting conversation. Only, when I went back to the kitchen, he was gone. No man. No one. I searched the house. I searched every room and corridor. I searched the garden. But still, there was no sign of him. And now, I watch the flames curl from out my window. I watch the conflagration consume my man and I am helpless. There is nothing I can do except stare at the horrid, sickening spectacle and watch as all I held dear, all I loved and cherished, is destroyed before my eyes.

Is life loss? Is this all there is? Each breath we exhale is a giving up, a death of life. I look around me, at the growing miasma of fetid crockery. At the dust spreading like bacteria on every piece of furniture. The dust which is my flesh, leaving me, a shedding of myself, shrinking so that I will fit, into my grave.

POETRY

BLAKE MORRISON

Old men sighing

I never understood it,
how in the places he most loved –
the car, say, or at the dinner table –
my father would stop talking and sigh,
and so long and low and sorrowfully,
like a dredger on a boating lake
bringing up sludge and weed.
Was it his death he was seeing?
Couldn't he guess how that made
the rest of us feel? Didn't he care?

Now like him I've started sighing
for no reason. Just that time when…
if only I'd…all the haunting almosts
and the one implacable was.

BLAKE MORRISON

© Mark Gerson

Latecomer

All I'm saying has been said before, but not by me.
To ourselves we're always new, like the sun coming up
Unaware it did so yesterday. The past might put us straight
But the past lives over the mountain, in a quiet meadow,
With horses grazing – horses we would recognize
If the stains on their flanks weren't hidden by trees.
Does the white mean they're getting old? Or is it the froth
From sweating saddles? We keep jostling for a better view
But can't get any closer than the quarry edge.
And really that's a kindness, like fog filling the valley
Or the man with the megaphone suddenly noticing
The crowds have left and there's no one to tell
That the track and field events are over for the day
And that all previous records will stand.

Wave

Remember the dream you had, in the chalet on top of the dunes –
how you woke on the sofabed to find the sea against the window,
the surface of the water higher than your eyes, as though you were staring
at a tank in an aquarium. You knew the water would rise and overwhelm you
but what you felt instead of fear was anger that you'd not seen this coming,
that no one had, the state-of-the-art early warning system having failed…
Then you were back before it began, down on the beach, reading the signals –

nothing obvious, just a pencil line at first, a scrawl on the horizon,

like arrested low cloud or a stubborn fog bank,
till you notice it's bigger than it was ten seconds since,

not a mountain but a range of foothills spanning the skyline,
a range you might speed across the desert to, by jeep,
but you've not moved, it's the foothills that are speeding to you

and though they're far-off you think you can hear something,
less a rumble than rising white noise, the hiss of a windsurfer
cutting through wake or the skitter of a dinghy with the wind at its back –
nothing clamorous, you could be lying on the beach and not notice

and people *are* lying on the beach, deep in a book or fast asleep,
it's only the paddlers in the shallows who've noticed something odd,
the tide drawing back, beating a retreat, *reculer pour mieux sauter*,
but the bathers don't speak French any more than you and though you've seen
tidal waves in picture books the thing coming at you looks different,

it's flatter and more insidious, with a bulge like the bulge in a spinnaker,
and what's worrying isn't the height but the weight, the miles of ocean
backing it up, for whereas most waves have a curl to their lip, as if just playing
or being ironic, there's a swell and gravity to this one, a seriousness that says
it means business, not like a wave that breaks enormously then withdraws,
exhausted from the effort, no, this wave will keep going, regardless –

two plates in the earth's crust set it off some white back, perhaps,
two plates overlapping each other like the shells of mating turtles,
or maybe a landslide caused it, or volcanic eruption, or nuclear bomb,

29

what the cause is you don't know but no dam or barrier can withstand it
and the sunbathers who've finally noticed can't hotfoot it to higher ground,
there are miles of marshland and coastal plain before the first hill,
and even a hill close by couldn't save them now, or you, it's too late for that,

because the waterwall is here, the sea-cliff, wave-mound, ocean-bore, surf-glut,
carrying fish and fishermen and all manner of wooden spars and snapoffs
from canoes, clippers, cutters, coracles, catamarans (every craft a hovercraft
when the wave first hit and threw it ahead but then pushed under in the crush
and pummelled to pieces), so that hulls, masts, beams, oars and paddles
are heading for you and even if they miss and you're not done for right off,
by a blow to the head from a keel or a crushing of ribs, the sheer force
will shove you down and you can forget those fancies you had of staying safe

inside the wave's clenched fist, the one miraculous survivor,
because the horizon's overtaking you and the sea with all its debris
sweeping you up and next thing you're inland half a mile in the marshes,
among the bulrushes, gently rocked and creeled in your reed basket,
where the rescue parties will later come looking, the Red Cross worker
with the mask over her face mistaking you for a crumpled grey sheet
then retching to find a body, a badly decomposed body needless to say,
though for you that's immaterial since you've long since ceased to be.

Yes this is the dream you had in the chalet, the one that keeps coming back,
whatever the weather, whichever the sea, even here, far from the Pacific,
on a summer's day by the east coast, where small breakers stroke the shingle
with a sigh and shush, the herring gulls quietly bobbing there like buoys,
'restful' you'd write if this were a church with a visitors' book,
except the calm could be the calm before a storm

                                              or the sea might keep on coming as it did
in '53, a thought to fill you with dread, though wouldn't wipeout in an instant
be better than this slow deletion, the loss of ground as the sea rises and the cliffs

are beaten back, and you receding in step, your bones thinning,
your hair whitening, and the thing that will kill you already triggered and on the move

but taking pains to stay hidden inside you, like a flood-tide hidden in the sea.

DAVID
CONSTANTINE

MEMOIR

WHERE I'M FROM, PART I

David Constantine

read in a history of Salford that Germanus and Patrick halted at the Gilda Brook and baptised the people there, at the Lady Well. That was in the fifth century. We used to pass the end or beginning of Gilda Brook Road, where it joins Eccles Old Road, every time we walked into Eccles, which was very often; but I don't remember the brook being visible at that place. Did it cross under the pavement and under the macadam? I remembered the name when I read about the two saints and guessed that the Gilda Brook, though I never knew it by any name, must have been the one that ran past a nursery on Victoria Road, and the water of it came back into my mind as sparkling and baptismal as I suppose it was a thousand and five hundred years ago. We crossed the stream where the houses ended, at the junction of Victoria Road and Orient Road, over a little bridge, into open fields, a limitless space where there were ponds. Nearer the nursery we went down to it, leaving the pavement, we went down a rough bank and the water was running quite rapidly at the bottom. We fished in it with jamjars, for creatures. There were green weeds and cresses. That was the place – so somebody said and I never doubted it – where a boy fell through the ice and swallowed his tongue. The last farm was near there, on Eccles Old Road, near where the Gilda Brook went under the traffic, I suppose, a farm set back between the large houses, the cattle were herded down a drive or lane, I remember them swinging along and a man in charge. Were they coming in from the fields?

I feel a particular pity for urban streams. They seem condemned to flow slowly, and to live for ever. They are at everybody's mercy. People will throw quite large objects – old prams, settees, bed-ends – into streams too small to have any hope, even in a flood, of ever submerging them. And all the harmful colours and the invisible poisons go down into them under our wheels and feet. But the Gilda Brook, wherever it was still to be seen, ran clear and supported little fish and tadpoles. In childhood there was only one other stream more beautiful, the one by St Mary's Church in Nefyn, behind the house we stayed in for our summer holidays; but that stream had every advantage, it came from a very near mountain and got pretty well unscathed into the sea.

The Gilda Brook was the boundary between Salford and Eccles. When my mother and father were married in 1940 they had no house of their own but lived in Salford with my grandmother, at 57 Liverpool Street. My father was away, with the Pioneer Corps in London, during the Blitz, on the Mile End Road. At Christmas Liverpool Street, near the ship canal, the docks and the railway, was badly bombed, a land mine fell close by, and they had to leave No. 57 and move in with Aunty Alice, in Birch Grove, Weaste. Then my mother got to hear of a house to rent. She took her chance, and that was the family house for thirty years: 13 Vestris Drive, Salford 6. It was in an area they knew already. My mother had gone there with the Girl Guides, for Sports Day in Swinton Fields; and when they were courting they would sometimes walk out into the fields to see the Sunshine Houses being built around Lancaster Road. You could secure one with a £5 deposit and buy it for £325. But that was more than they could manage.

The move from Liverpool Street to Birch Grove to Vestris Drive was a move out – out of the long street of the gasworks and the abattoirs, out of the densely packed terraces with b; yards, outside toilets, back alleys, into the new drives where houses had decent little front gardens and generous long t ones and where there were trees, very many trees, and exter fields close by. There were no trees at all on Liverpool Street no gardens, only bits of black park; and where Aunty liv Weaste, though the streets were called groves and namec trees – Birch Grove, Ash Grove, Myrtle Grove – there w trees except at the doctor's surgery which stood in a large grounds and was called The Willows, and except in the cemetery. But the shortest way from Birch Grove to Vestris Drive was through the allotments and the fields.

Eccles Old Road, where it concerned us, had come down Buile Hill and was running level and very busy westwards along our southern edge, though I never thought in terms of north, south, east and west. You could feel its cobbles through the coats of tar and see the old tramlines. Along one side, the right as you went into Eccles, it had enormous houses which, when they were built, must have stood in open country with their gardens. The road then was known as Millionaires' Road; but the million-aires had gone elsewhere and their family mansions had been parcelled into flats or had become nursing homes, a blind home, a doctor's surgery, a private hotel. I remember these houses as black, except one on the hill, said to be haunted and called The Rookery, which was a sooty red. Lancaster Road turns off Eccles Old Road opposite Hope Church and goes straight for nine tenths of a mile (we measured it when we got mileometers on our bikes), and the big houses sent off a spur along it, on the lefthand side, for about a quarter of its way. In the new housing, in avenues and drives mostly beginning with 'V' (Vestris, Voltaire, Vauban, Vandyke, Victoria …), we were in the angle of Lancaster Road and Eccles Old Road, and the ancient black mansions, with their trees and stables and mostly derelict gardens and grounds, gave us a territory. Many gardens came together at the back of our house. On the right ours ran to a point with the neighbour's and next-door-but-one's, and on the left they came in from houses which, if you followed the pavements, were some distance away; and all these quite new gardens reached to the borders of the old and ruinous grounds of the big houses on Lancaster Road. We looked down the garden at trees: a row of small black poplars in Hopkins's on our left, two tall Lombardy poplars just inside our bottom fence, and in Jones's, next-door-but-one's, where it reached our garden at its extreme angle, there were three or four very large black poplars, and trees of that size edged and divided the gardens of the old mansions and lined Lancaster Road where the big double-decker buses hit against them. The trees had survived the new housing when it came. They are to me, because of their blackness and when I think of their roots, like entrances into the underworld. We climbed over our bottom fence into a passage which ran alongside Jones's and gave a back access to the houses on Lancaster Road. It ended where our garden ended in a pair of garages that were mostly left open and unused. This was a good place to meet and begin something. We got over our bottom fence under the Lombardy and the black (or Manchester) poplars and went where we liked, on ways we devised, along the limits of the private gardens, climbing their broken walls, squeezing through their railings, entering their stable yards and outbuildings. At nights we heard the owls.

After the very big houses on Lancaster Road, after their trees and their darkness, there was a short row of modern ones, set back; then, still on the left, the big open space of De La Salle playing fields. These were below the level of the pavement and the road, so that when we climbed on to their fence, which we almost always did, to balance along it, the drop on the left, into the fields, was greater, increasingly, than the drop on the right to the pavement. The top beam, though it had soft spots and troughs in it where the wood had rotted despite the creosote, was wide enough for most of its long length, and we ran along pretty quickly; but at the far end it thinned, and balancing there, since there the drop was greatest, took a bit more nerve. That corner was particular. We spent time jumping off the top rail into the field. I liked jumping from heights. I had a dream of a level mattress world where, in pyjamas, you could bounce very high and fall without any harm. I retained for some years the wish, almost the belief, that I could fly, and practised this possibility by repeatedly jumping off the wall of our front garden over the privet hedge on to the patch of lawn. The trick was to stay in the air as long as possible by jumping high and kicking and pedalling with the legs. But in the far corner of De La Salle playing fields the drop was so great that we dared not increase it by jumping higher. We went down crouching and hit the ground hard. That corner had trees, a row of the usual Manchester poplars, along the fields' border with the gardens of Orient Road. You could trespass through the fields – around the edge or, in a fright, across the pitches themselves – to the fence, a vertical hoarding, on Wilton Road, which was the north-south vertical line, parallel to Lancaster Road, of what we called the Block. On the corner where we did our frightening jumps the last house of Orient Road had been bombed away.

School was just across the road, but I am thinking of fields and therefore keeping on the left and going a few hundred yards further up Lancaster Road, past Orient and Oxford and all their connecting 'O's (Orlanda, Otranto, Ormonde, Odessa and Orme) to an opening between the houses and a dirt track that led into Matheson Playing Fields. I have layers of later interest in those fields, but what they were first and are still when I bring them back to mind, is space. They went over into Swinton Fields, which were limitless. Space, two planes, the grass and the sky, and my feeling is not as it might have been, as it was elsewhere and later more than once, of being lost and at a terrible distance, but of closeness and of being loved and happy and entirely safe. We must have gone there for walks when I was really very small and set up a little camp among the grasses which we called silver-spoons. It is the loveliest word to come out of my childhood, and peculiar. The sun was in the flowering spray of the grasses, silvery red, and there were skylarks, going up like jets of water, higher and higher, and holding, and the song cascading down. Later we flew kites in the fields and model aircraft, and set off across them on bikes to find the ponds. I am sure that my mother and father were very happy when we all went into the fields together. Once we watched my father playing cricket there for his office team. I remember him coming in to bowl, so concentrated, fit and fast. When we could face up to him, on a beach where there was plenty of room, he would bowl against us like that.

In our area when we were children the housing was not deep. Perhaps it was only one row deep, along the road, and you passed through a gap between the houses and immediately entered somewhere else. Vestris Drive went into Voltaire Avenue and Voltaire Avenue reached Lancaster Road and across that road a passage cut through the semis into the Camp. During the War it had been an army camp, later it was built on and became the Fairhope Estate, but for some time it existed as a wilderness: pits, trenches, brick walls, pillboxes, the broken huts, the concrete bases, going under the weeds. The tallest weed was the bombsite flower, the rosebay willowherb. We went in looking for bonfire wood, and there were other gangs. It felt riskier than trespassing, the owners had gone, you were left to your own devices in the badlands. The Camp was not like the park or the playing fields or the allotments, but uneasier, the name excited me, going in there was a braver expedition. The semis on Lancaster Road were very respectable, but they had the Camp behind them and a way between them into it.

You could get through the Camp to Eccles Old Road, opposite Buile Hill Park. On its borders, which were the limit of any foray in that direction, the houses were immense and eerie. There was the haunted Rookery, and a Hall that was being pulled down. Later they built the Secondary Modern there. We peered in through the rhododendrons, and sneaked up the long private drives. These borders are particularly attractive and elusive in my memory now, like the zone just before sleeping when the mind unravels among the images. I can remember no limit for the playing fields, only flatness, the silverspoons, the sky, and, somewhere very far distant, the ponds; but the Camp, which the adult world had given up, ended in a privacy that was malign and derelict and that we spied on through the sooty leaves and crept into as far as we dared. We pushed forward as the great Hall was demolished, into its ruined space, in among the rubble and the timbers, until they built the school and all the territory shrank and was obliterated.

There was no traffic in our drive and avenue when we were small, or none to speak of, and we played our games where we felt like playing them, to and fro across the road (in the cold winters we made ice slides down it). We might cross Lancaster Road ourselves, taking care, but never Eccles Old Road, which for those days was always busy, especially in the rush hour which we were warned about as though the danger of it would reach us wherever we were. My grandmother gripped me very tightly by the hand when we crossed that road to get into the allotments behind Hope Church and through them to Aunty Alice's in Birch Grove. I wish by a dream I could do the walk again, just once, there and back, and have it all come back to me and every yard of it be in my mind for a while at least. We went in at the church and where we came out again we were only a few yards away from Aunty's house. Entering and arriving are still clear to me, the two ends, but everything between them has been lost, except a sense, a love of allotments, especially allotments along a railway line, an intense and childish love of coltsfoot, which I picked to give Aunty when we reached her house, and of Michaelmas daisies at the other end of the year, and the love of my grandmother which I took as much for granted as I did the terrain itself, the ground, the path, the air. I've stood at either end, by the church, which is now among housing, and by the ragged curtailment of Birch Grove, and tried by force of looking and straining with the memory to get back in, and could not, cannot, though it is certainly all still in me, every one of the scores and scores of walks, under concrete now and other people's houses and gardens, under their traffic and their families, but in me still in the way that these things matter, as love and loyalty and gratitude. When I went back grown-up and from far away, though Aunty's house had gone there was still a gate into a thin remnant of allotments. Often I have stood in trains, at the open window, and taken a bearing on the spire of the church and tried my best, passing at speed, to get the path to come to me. But then the railway line was reduced, for a motorway, and the street, Birch Grove, has shrunk almost to nothing.

When my mother and father rented the house in Vestris Drive and began their married life there they were moving out of the working-class housing of Seedley and Weaste into something that was newer and less defined, more open and likely to facilitate change; but a great deal of our lives for most of the time that we lived in Vestris Drive harked back to the older inner zone of Salford. My grandmother moved with my parents to the new house, and since my father, and for periods my mother too, was out at work, she looked after us and did much of the house-keeping. There were shops on Orient Road and also on Eccles Old Road not far distant, but she preferred to walk to Weaste, through the allotments and, when they were built on, through the new estate, to the butcher's, fishmonger's, greengrocer's and the Co-op, and I went with her often, and we called at Aunty's in Birch Grove. Our doctor's was in Weaste too, at the Willows, as was the cemetery where Aunty Alice's baby is buried and which Gran visited regularly in memory of her husband who was killed in France and not buried anywhere. We went swimming in Seedley Baths, we went to Cross Lane Market, and we visited cousins in Buckingham Avenue, up the railway line from Birch Grove, by Winterbottom's Paper Works. Nothing that had to do with the family held us to the new housing around Vestris Drive, everything went back, across the old road, into Weaste and further into Manchester, or across Manchester to Denton where Aunty Ev and Uncle Arthur lived (in a caretaker's flat belonging to a mineral factory). It was a bit different on my father's side – George was an officer in the RAF, away, and Harry had moved 'down south', as a travelling salesman – but Gladys still lived in the old housing in Stockport and my father's mother, Grandma Con, lived alone, in some disrepute, in Broughton. We visited her and Gladys too and our cousins in Denton in the pop factory, but the greatest pull was back to Weaste, Cross Lane and Regent Road, back towards Liverpool Street. From our house in Vestris Drive we could hear the roar of the match at the Willows ground and the hooter blow at Winterbottom's for the dinner break and knocking-off; but Gran there with us was in a very different place from where her sister, our Gran West, still lived next door to Winterbottom's, in Buckingham Avenue (though both were in Salford 6, which always seemed odd to me).

Birch Grove was altogether different from Vestris Drive. The house, the last but two of a terrace, had a back yard which let out into an unpaved alley shared by the back yards of the next street along (another grove). The women slung the alley with their washing. I remember a very little area, as though we never dared to go far away. We never made any friends who might have taken us into the proper territory, and Aunty Alice and Uncle Norman were childless. We stayed close. The street itself was cobbled. I chased the pigeons across it, trying to put salt on their tails. They ran away. There were no pigeons in Vestris Drive. Or we stayed inside, and went upstairs into the spare back bedroom which smelled of creosote and sawn wood. Uncle Norman worked for the Post Office, on telephone lines, and could get himself lengths of pole for firewood when one was taken down, and he stored the lengths, along with all the things from his years at sea, in the spare bedroom, which would have been their child's had the baby lived. In that room I was as happy as Aladdin. Otherwise, if we went out, we stood at the fencing along the railway line and watched for trains through cracks and knot-holes. There was a station a little way up, but the biggest trains went through without stopping, into Manchester or away to Crewe and North Wales, their speed shook the fence and the houses. At Buckingham Avenue the house was the last on the terrace, closest to the railway line, and bricks were being shaken loose in the gable end. In that household there were three children – Keith, Elaine and Michael – and we played with them, but still the area was never homely. We looked through the railings into Winterbottom's reservoirs. In one the water was hot, it steamed, in another it was swimming with red goldfish. There was something wrong in our cousins' house which we were never told about. The adults were wrong. Uncle John sat by the fire, he held out his hands to the warmth, he was sick in some consumptive way and his face showed it. His face was white and it went in at the mouth. Aunty Edna had good looks. In any comparison with our grandmother, Gran West, her sister, came off worst. The house smelled very differently from ours. We went there on Christmas Morning, first to Birch Grove then to Buckingham Avenue, to exchange presents. We had to dress up. Did they like us coming dressed up into their house? We were kept cleaner than Keith, Elaine and Michael. Children notice these things: who at school smells of piss and has a snotty nose, whose house is not as it should be, these distinctions will be remembered for ever, and others too: whose mother wore too much scent and make-up, whose father smelled of beer, who talked posh. The rag-and-bone man came round Vestris Drive with a horse and cart, he gave his peculiar cry – Ragbone! Sambone! – and we ran out with whatever we had and got a brownstone in exchange. But I'm sure that neither we nor anyone else in the new avenues and drives ever brownstoned the step, so we must have taken it to Aunty in Birch Grove, who did.

Vestris Drive was a respectable area, the houses were semi-detached, the families had more space, their troubles were kept in greater privacy. Except next door to us, the Hopkins's, they carried on in a way that was not respectable. They were our other half, in the other semi, we had a party wall and, looking down the garden, the lefthand fence in common. They had been bombed out of their home in Patricroft, the house in Vestris Drive was requisitioned for them, and they never left. Enid and Terry were the youngest children, and above them, rising into the adult world, Angela, Shirley, Brian, Reggie and Kevin. Father drank, and the oldest boys grew up to join him in it, we heard the raised voices coming through the wall and sometimes the noise of fighting, crashes and heavy falls, once very clearly 'Tie the bugger up!', as they restrained the dad. Mrs Hopkins flung out of the house in the middle of the night, slammed the door, stood in the road and screamed she was going to her mother's. This was no way to carry on in Vestris Drive. The Hopkins garden was a wilderness, all long grass, and they never mended the fence. Ours was upkept properly, the garden and the house, my father was always busy keeping them nice, cutting the privets, painting the windows and the gutters etc, etc, he never stopped, but Hopkins let theirs go to rack and ruin. I liked the place, and we were not forbidden to go in, I played with Terry and Enid. I went in once and found all the floorboards up, you had to balance along the joists, there was a deep black drop below. And that is how I came to think of the house, as a place where you had to manage without the floorboards. In our own sometimes we rearranged the furniture and tried to get around without ever putting a foot on the carpet, which we said was the sea; but the crazy challenge of the Hopkins's house was permanent. And in there also Mrs Hopkins or one of the older girls might give me a sugar butty, they seemed to live off them. Above a pit, in the smell of the earth that every house rests on, I bit through the soft slices, the sugar scrunched between my teeth and melted in my mouth. Kevin went to sea and Reggie and Brian after him, they brought strange presents with them when they came home on leave, a blue hare, which they kept in the ruinous shed by the side of the house, and a brilliant cockatoo. I climbed the poplars in their garden after caterpillars, fell out of a tree by the shed and broke my arm. When Enid, sitting on the fence, told me I would go to hell since I wasn't a Catholic, I pushed her off. Terry said once when we were playing on the front with something my father had made for me that he wished he had a father who made him things. They were the loyalest family. The father quietened down. The children, when they married, always came home to visit, bringing their babies. I remember the old man last as a whitehaired peaceable grandfather.

When I went back and stood at the bottom of our garden (as I have often done in my dreams), it was as poor and overgrown as Hopkins's ever was and the fence between the two had largely fallen down. And how small it looked, but in my childhood it was long and spacious. My memory crowds into it everything that was ever there and everything we ever did. The lawn, with a crazy paving down the middle, only went half way, to a sundial and a rustic trellis that stood from fence to fence. Beyond were the raspberries, gooseberries, strawberries and blackcurrants, and then a wild area, under the poplar trees. There we did as we liked: lit fires and cooked an outdoor meal; built a house, properly roofed and glazed, and lived in it; rode on enormous branches lopped from the black poplars (they stood on legs like beasts, they put out stumps like horns); made a cricket pitch; got through into the passage. Just inside this lower half, by the rustic, my father had made a shallow rectangular concrete paddling pool, that hedgehogs came to. I loved the rowan on Jones's side, its berries – I have the feeling that I must have eaten them, their orange-red, the weight and at first the coolness of a cluster in the hands, their flesh and smell, surely with every sense at once or during the years we ingest whatever we love. I have taken some things in as the landscape did the blood and shreds of Orpheus. When we buried things in tins it was mostly in the lower half of the garden. I remember exactly where I tried to bury smoke (and how it resisted, like any living creature). In the other half, near the house, we still played cricket, and tried to lift the shots harmlessly over the rustic into the wild part. Everywhere since I have looked for the red roses that grew on the trellis and the fences, and never found their kind. Birthday parties on the lawn. Building ships, aeroplanes, locomotives with furniture and boxes. The bonfire left two semi-circles either side the path, which my father seeded and they grew again softly, and again were blackened.

I had uneasy feelings about one place in the upper part of the garden, close by the righthand fence where the rustic joined it. There in the border a pipe three or four inches across and threaded like a screw on the outside stuck up out of the ground. Though it was choked with soil I believed it went down to where something horrible lived, that might always come up through it, into our garden. At times when I was fearful I hardly dared go beyond the rustic into the lower half. When we were warned at school never to go with strangers the fear of it happening possessed me completely. I dared myself to go as far down the garden as the rowan tree. And I made things worse by doing, on this subject, what I was prone to do on any subject: I invented a tale and told it for the truth. I said a man had stopped me on the way home from school and tried to take me away. And saying it to my mother I believed it and was scared of the garden in its lower part because easily someone might come up the passage and over the bottom fence. Then I had a dream: at exactly the point where our garden came together and ended with Jones's I was held and my Aunty Alice thrust a long knife into my heart. For some days I gave myself up to being murdered.

We were at Nefyn, the paradisal place. I came round the rocks at the far end of the beach. It was a sort of breakwater where we fished for crabs and blennies. Some boys were there, bigger than me, they had caught a few crabs and on a slab of rock they were smashing their shells with pebbles. I felt then and still the inadequacy of the carapace. I watched, I didn't intervene.

We had a boy in our class whose father was a slaughterman. He said he could arrange for the class to visit the abattoir. Our teacher said it would not be for the squeamish. I was sure we would go and that I would not dare admit to being squeamish. The abattoir was at the end of Liverpool Street, the herds were driven along the road. I lived in a sick dread of being taken into the place itself and obliged to watch. Others in the class wer looking forward to it.

My father drowned a mouse in a bucket of water. This is the one and only cruelty that comes to mind when I think of him. The bucket full of water stood on the kitchen floor, again and again the mouse paddled rapidly upwards to the surface and with the rake we used to rake the hearth out my father again and again pushed the creature down. In my memory now, staring into the bucket of water, there is no end, the mouse climbs up for air, my father prods it down.

An old man used to sit on a bench outside the Home on Eccles Old Road. He sat there shaking uncontrollably and a very white spittle ran out of his mouth. His body was twisted, his hands were held up like paws; but it was his mouth I mainly looked at when I passed. I couldn't help looking. I can still see his face.

I was playing in the drive with Nicky Lamb, Big Jean and Pat Chadderton. They said there had been an accident near Cross Lane. They said a man had been run over and that his skin was wrapped around the wheels of the vehicle that had done it. In the afternoon I was taken shopping to Cross Lane by my mother and my gran. As we got nearer to where I supposed the thing had happened, I hung back. I imagined that the skin had fitted the wheels like tyres, giving them a peculiar softness and silence. I did not admit what I was frightened of seeing, but hung back. They bought me a cream bun to encourage me along.

A man was killed on a building site on Cholmondeley Road. A lorry backed over his head. In school they were saying you could see the large stain it had made on the dirt track into the site.

In childhood the worst was never telling anyone. I stuck for days in the conviction that I should suffer or witness something which would overwhelm me with fear and pity.

Continues on p.116

IAN McMILLAN

Reading At Fifty

It's cold outside. Breath visible in clouds
Of examined air that wait for a moment, then
Saunter away; the date is one you'd ring
In a diary or rather the date is one I'd
Ring in a diary: 21st of January 2006.

I'm fifty years old today. It's cold outside
Like it was when I was born, and I'm sitting
Reading on the rocking chair in our conservatory
And maybe I'm dreaming. I'm fifty
And here comes my grandson Thomas

Carrying a sack as big as his two-year-old
Self. It's a sack full of words and sentences,
All the words and sentences I've read
In the last half-century and it's not heavy
It's lighter than our breath in the freezing air.

We tip the words out on the floor by the toybox
And the sentences stand up like Sentence-henges
And the paragraphs make paragraphscapes
That spread over the carpet as though they are
Spilled soup which really they are, the spilled

Page-soup of fifty years of reading. In my dream
We play with those read words and laugh and we laugh
And then Thomas, with a grave face like a mystic,
Reveals another sack as big as the first one
Or bigger. Much bigger. Here is your reading

For the next fifty years he says and he tips
Out a mountain, a range of word-mountains
And we sit and we read alone and together
For the next fifty years and the reading is growing
And the reading is growing and the reading

The reading, the reading is endless. And warming.

FRANK COTTRELL BOYCE

WHAT I LEARNED FROM THE 2012 OLYMPICS

Frank Cottrell Boyce

Fifteenth Roscoe Lecture Series, LJMU,
St George's Hall, Liverpool, Thursday 4th October 2012

What did I learn from the 2012 Olympics? I learned that we're a better nation than we thought we were; more inclusive and more creative, and more rambunctious and more up-for-it, and a more well-organised nation than we thought we were.

The first London Games were in 1908. They were organised by a guy called Lord Desborough, who had only heard about the Games two years before. The fabulous stadium he built at White City has the swimming pool in the middle of the running track, a vast, unheated pool. In 1908 Britain was of course the centre of an empire, so it was basically us against the rest of the world, and we *were* half the world. It was a needle game between us and the USA, who hated the empire and monarchy, and the climax of that struggle was the marathon. There were 100,000 people in the stadium to watch the end of the marathon, a face-off between two great athletes: Johnny Hayes, an Irish American, and Tom Longboat, a Native American, who was running for Canada and therefore for the Empire. Tom Longboat dropped out with a few miles to go. He had cramp but his coach claimed that Tom had been nobbled with strychnine. The doctors who were attending said it was more likely that the problem was caused by the bottles of champagne that he'd been chugging all the way round. Johnny Hayes went on for a few miles longer because he was cunning and he didn't drink the champagne. He just gargled brandy. He dropped out with about a mile to go. So there were 100,000 people waiting in the stadium, and then a figure comes into the arena and it's not Johnny Hayes and it's not Tom Longboat; it's this tiny figure in red shorts, a guy called Dorando Pietri. When Pietri came into the stadium he staggered back, shaken by the force of crowd's cheer. He could barely stand

"Stories survive"

and eventually after stumbling round the track he did collapse and was helped over the line by British judges and therefore disqualified. But there was uproar on his behalf because he'd been so valiant and he'd struggled against the limits of his own body, so the Queen gave him a special cup. That story survives. The Empire has fallen, the White City that they built for that stadium has gone, but the story of Dorando Pietri is still alive even though it's not the story that anyone would have expected to come out of those Games; it's not a story about American supremacy or British supremacy, or about supermen and fantastic bodies. It's a story about weakness and a story, I think, that shows the potency of stories. Stories survive. Stories survive longer than empires, longer than Games, longer than the people that other people spend money on, but it's very difficult to control what stories come out.

Of course going into our Games we were in an atmosphere of incredible negativity. We'd worked two-and-a-half years on the opening ceremony – I don't know if anyone will remember this now – and in the months before the Games, the negativity around the ceremony was extraordinary. We got the most hateful press. People would look at me with sympathy when I said I was working on the opening ceremony of the Olympic Games.

To refresh your memory here are some comments from the online edition of the *Daily Mail*: 'This is going to be a huge embarrassment with the eyes of the world upon us, falling about with laughter'. Signed 'Fed-up Taxpayer, UKIP all the way', and he gives his address as 'Plymouth, EUSSR'. 'This will be the worst ceremony in history. I'm glad it's happening in London'. Signed 'Paul, Leeds'. When we moved into the stadium we rehearsed with the 7000 volunteers on the Saturdays building up to it. It rained on nearly every one of those Saturdays and, for every one of those Saturdays, we had the *Daily Mail* helicopter floating above the stadium taking pictures, and *Daily Mail* stooges outside the stadium offering money to people for spoilers from the ceremony. It was a diagram of everything that could be wrong with a society – here were 7000 people doing something for nothing and here were people paying a fortune to spoil it for them.

Giles Coren from the *Times*, bless him, filed his copy just as the ceremony was starting. He wrote this excoriating review and then twenty minutes in he realised that it was all wrong and he rewrote his article. Sitting in the stadium, he rewrote and re-filed his article, but too late for the early editions. 'I'm in the slightly embarrassing position…' he wrote, 'depending on where you live in the country you've got a piece by me saying "This is a load of inflated nonsense and a waste of money", or if you live in some other part of the country you've got me saying, "This is the greatest night of my life. If we don't win a single medal, it won't matter. Because we had this"'. That's my first lesson from the Olympic Games: if you can lower people's expectations, it will help. And the lesson from that is that there's a huge disconnect in this country between the press and what's really happening. The more profound lesson is not to be afraid and if you feel that you're doing something extraordinary push on with it and don't worry.

Danny Boyle did not blink during those weeks. We did not have one single meeting about what to do about that terrible press. Not one. Nobody said, 'What are we going to do? How are we going to spin this?' Everyone just carried on. For me, the moment that changed everything was walking back up to Bromley-by-Bow Station one night. For the preceding two years that had been the loneliest, most desperate walk along the side of a dual carriageway. It's really bleak. But on this night I was swamped by volunteers who had just finished their rehearsal, thousands of them. Every one of them had a big grin. They were every age, every class, every race, every level of ability – all giggling in their little teams and full of the spirit of what we were doing. They piled onto the train and got off at various stations on the Central Line along the way, and it made me think of that great poem by Philip Larkin, 'The Whitsun Weddings'. It's a poem about a train journey from Hull to London at Whitsuntide; lots of newly-weds pile onto the train. He's writing about the brides setting off on their new life at the end of their journey: 'And what [that train] held stood ready to be loosed with all the power that being changed can give'. He has that line, 'the frail, travelling coincidence'. Maybe that's the next lesson for me as an artist, as a filmmaker and a creative person – that what a great work of art really does is bring people together. It's not about the content. It's about providing enough of a pretext to bring all kinds of different people together in a spirit that's not competitive.

"The opening ceremony had the atmosphere of a school nativity play"

Shortly after that we moved into the stadium for rehearsals and then it always felt like that. You'd walk through the park which had its dystopian aspect. This was a big corporate venture: you had the biggest McDonald's in the world; there were Rapier missiles defending it; there was G4S security everywhere. But when you got into the stadium, it was as though Danny had created this mini utopia of people who were doing something because they wanted to in the spirit of fellowship and fun.

The night of the opening ceremony – although it was a huge event that went out all around the world – had the atmosphere of a school nativity play. I remember sitting with Rick Smith from Underworld who did the music, and, as the athletes were marching out, he said, 'They're slowing down, Frank. I'm going to go and up the beats'. He was getting the drummers to chivvy them on, and it felt like getting your kids on to stage. That would be another lesson for me from 2012: how do you motivate people? We've lived in a country and an atmosphere and an ideology that says to get the best out of people – to get the best people – you have to pay the most money. My lesson coming out of those games is that I was surrounded by people who were not motivated by money at all, who were doing an amazing job because they believed in something; or because they thought it would be fun, and they did amazing work, whereas there were big companies, like G4S, who were paid phenomenal amounts of money, who totally cocked up. Maybe when we go out with that big pay cheque, looking for the best people, we're systematically selecting the worst. It's not just that we're paying them too much but the people who can be paid – whose motive is money – are treacherous; the money is a distraction.

On to the third thing that I learned, the most important thing, which I already knew but which really came home to me: the importance of books. Boyd Tonkin, writing for the *Independent*, reviewed the opening ceremony and said, 'Literature won gold at Stratford last night', because that opening ceremony was marinated in literature and spiked with quotations from Milton, and from Shakespeare, and from Blake, Mary Poppins, Harry Potter – all this stuff from books that was in there. It wasn't really just what we *took* from books so much as the *process* that we had. For the first six or seven months of working on the ceremony we didn't do anything that I would recognise as work at all. I came with my laptop and sat there, ready to take notes, and Danny said – there were only four of us at the time – 'I don't want you to write anything down. I don't want any notes taken. For the first few months we're just going to share what we think is good'. For the first few months we went into that little room in Soho and stuck things on the wall including the G. K. Chesterton phrase, 'We are perishing for want of wonder, not for want of wonders'. Great phrases such as that became my aesthetic. Muhammad Ali: 'Float like a butterfly, sting like a bee'. A great quotation from Jesse Owen: 'Find the good. It's all around you. Find it, showcase it and you'll start believing it', an amazing thing for him to have said because after the 1936 Olympics he barely ran again, snubbed by the American establishment. My favourite Olympic quotation is from Jim Thorpe, a Native American athlete who won gold for the decathlon and pentathlon when it was in Sweden. He was an astonishing athlete: a footballer, basketball player, runner – everything. He was an all-round amazing athlete and, when he got his gold medal, King Gustav said to him, 'Sir, I believe you are the greatest athlete the world has ever seen,' and Jim Thorpe said, 'Thanks, King'.

Auden said that literature is the only way that we ever break bread with the dead. I think what we really gained wasn't any of these little things that we actually used, but a sense of being able to break out of the prison of the present – literature opens you out to other times and other ways of thinking. If we stay trapped in the present, our options are limited but once you read you're thinking in a completely different way; you're engaging with a set of voices that you don't hear anywhere else. Only books can do this. I love films; I've given my life to films; I love theatre; I love the opening ceremony, but all these are created by a particular kind of person, a person who's affable, cunning, self-confident, but books can be written by *anybody*. Some of the most important books in the history of the world were written by slaves; by people who could barely speak to other people; who were de-socialised; by prisoners. Only in books do you hear those voices from the margin and yet it is from those margins that the greatest ideas come.

The most important book we read was a book by a guy called Humphrey Jennings, a great British filmmaker in the Second World War, a propaganda filmmaker who wrote an astonishing book, *Pandæmonium*, which is clippings of eyewitness reports of the Industrial Revolution. It has diary extracts and bills of trade and newspaper reports and poems. When you hold it in your hand it feels as though it's buzzing. *Pandæmonium* is not a continuous book with a conclusion to offer. It's just these extracts: 'This is incredibly exciting, I've invented the Spinning Jenny' followed by a girl saying, 'This is terrible, I've got to work on the Spinning Jenny all day'. The power of that kind of collage, that 'frail, travelling coincidence,' became the model for the opening ceremony. We don't have to decide what our national identity is. We *are* all these contradictions and they all work together.

The story of that book takes me to the next lesson. The origin of that book was that Humphrey Jennings was making a film in South Wales, during the Second World War, *The Silent Village*, and he had to stay in this village in South Wales called Cwmgiedd for about five or six months. As a thank-you for the hospitality they showed him, he gave a series of lectures which became the book. So it was a gift originally. It was a present. I first came across the book when someone gave it to me, and then I gave it to Danny Boyle when he was making a play out of *Frankenstein* years later. I said, 'You must read *Pandæmonium*, because it's got all this stuff about electricity, galvanism, all the things that are in Frankenstein. I'll get it you for Christmas'. I hadn't realised it had been out of print for a very long time so when I went onto Amazon to buy it, it cost me 50 quid. I was generous enough to buy this book, but I wasn't generous enough not to mention how expensive it had been.

He said, 'Thank-you very much'.

I said, 'That cost me 50 quid, so you'd better read it'.

Gifts are unpredictable in a way that other things are not. You don't know what the consequences are going to be. There's always something reckless, something courageous about generosity. The Olympics is about personal excellence; winning a race; beating somebody else – but every single time those athletes came in, they thanked their mums and dads, or their PE teachers, their children, their trainers, and so you can't help but be aware that every achievement is floating on this raft of generosity – and on a generosity that has no agenda. Danny was very keen that there'd be no interpretation – the ceremony wouldn't be left-wing or right-wing. The key thing was that everybody in the nation shared it. It belonged to everybody.

The last lesson is about choosing wisely. I've told you about the potency of stories. If we choose the wrong story, we can get trapped inside the wrong world and terrible things can happen. I don't need to say that in Liverpool because this summer we've seen the unravelling of the Hillsborough story, and for me the most abiding image of that is a line of fit, young policemen standing across the middle of the pitch, looking at the disaster as it unfolded and not moving a muscle because they literally could not see what was happening in front of them, trapped in a narrative of pitch invasion and football hooliganism. They were literally hypnotised by the story. We have to choose our stories and to ask ourselves: are we believing the right stories about our nation? Are we believing the right stories about our city? Because a nation, and a city, is not a shared history; it's not a way of talking or a way of dressing: it is a project. It's a journey we're all travelling together. It is the frail, travelling coincidence.

PHILLIP JUPITUS

© Andy Hollingworth

POETRY

PHILLIP JUPITUS

The Sailor Of Bari

Raised in Qandala
On fish and rice
And tales of Dhegdheer
Nadif eventually fetched up
Just off Old Compton Street
In a mucky book shop
His lean sinewy body hunched
All elbows and shoulders
A three bar electric fire
Humming with the effort
Tanning the back of his Wranglers

While physically motionless
Nadif's mind whirls
With nines, threes, sixes and sevens
The bashed Nokia
Waltzes across the counter
Like a punch drunk wasp
He recognises the shattered number
And answers his manager's call

'Mister Harris!'
'We've had a complaint Nadif...'
The seven goes there
So that must be a nine
'Yes?'

'A punter. Asked you for some animal stuff.'
'Yes.'
'You sold him *Life On Earth*...'
Three
Three
And three
'I did.'
'Then when he asked for girl on girl
You sold him the 1975 *Bunty* Annual...'
That can't be a four there
'That is also correct...'
'He meant the girl stuff and the animal stuff downstairs!'
'I see. That is unfortunate.'
Pause
Six
'Has he asked for his money back?'
'What?'
'Has the customer asked for his money back?'
'Well... No.'
'Then what is the problem Mister Harris?'
'Fair point Nadif. Good lad. Take a fiver out the till.'
'Thank you mister Harris.'

Absently pushing the red button
Nadif fits the last three numbers
Into his Sudoku
And throws the paper away
Before taking a crisp twenty pound note
Out of the till
And below the aquiline nose
An even beautiful
Snow-white smile
Sparks out of his dark angular face
'This is so much easier than piracy...'
He says aloud
Before turning back
To his fire damaged copy
Of *Treasure Island*

FROM *THE ANTI-ROMANTIC CHILD*

Priscilla Gilman

The Anti-Romantic Child is a memoir that has won great acclaim in the States and was called 'smart, soulful, and involving' by Nick Hornby in the *Believer* magazine. It is currently unpublished in the UK. Priscilla Gilman was a high-flying academic at Yale, specialising in the poetry of Wordsworth. At the same time, married to Richard, a fellow academic in literature, she sought to realise the Wordsworthian ideal of childhood in her own new-born son, Benjamin. From the first, the child seemed exceptionally gifted, compulsively attracted to both words and numbers. The two excerpts that follow, however, trace the first realisation that something is wrong.

During the most uncertain time after 9/11, Richard and I would continually say, 'At least we have Benj', or 'Good old Benj'. Benj was the sure thing, the bedrock, the fulcrum of our lives, the meaning of our lives, really. And then, just a few months later, as the evaluations began, the child I thought I knew was gone. Benj had been our refuge from the storm, our unadulterated, uncomplicated, simple joy. And then suddenly he *was* the storm, he was complicated and confusing and terrifyingly at risk.

One of the most painful things about those first days was that I was being made to feel that all the things I'd considered unique and special about Benj were instead uncontrollable manifestations of a disorder. He was not unusual; he was typical, ordinary, a classic case. He didn't have an interesting mind; he had faulty wiring. He didn't have a distinctive personality; he had a syndrome. His jubilant recitations of Robert Frost's 'Fire and Ice' and 'Nothing Gold Can Stay' and word- and note-perfect renditions of many of the songs from *The Sound of Music*, *West Side Story*, and *Oklahoma!* were not the result of a love or appreciation for poetry or music but rather a mindless parroting. His animated recitation of scripts from *Between the Lines* and *Sesame Street* was not a dazzling display of his powers of memory so much as it was 'perseveration', 'echolalia', 'video talk', and was to be discouraged. His ability to line up his letter blocks in alphabetical order and to make number chains from 1 to 20 was a compulsion, not a pleasure. His seeing letters everywhere – in the shape of

"In my darkest moments, I saw Benjamin as a textbook case, an embodiment of a syndrome"

his food (a string of spaghetti was an *S*) or the curve and lines of a piece of jewellery (little earrings of mine were *T*s, a linked bracelet I had was seven *O*s) – wasn't perceptive or imaginative – these were ominous signs of obsession. His not responding to questions or not turning his head in response to a voice wasn't a sign of single-minded focus on an engrossing activity so much as it was an inability to engage with the outside world. His early reading wasn't 'just like his mom'; his perfectionism wasn't 'just like his father', or at least not in any reassuring way. Both were symptoms, items on a checklist, pathologies. In my darkest moments, that is to say, I saw Benjamin as a textbook case, an embodiment of a syndrome rather than a distinctive individual. In those first days of questioning who he was and what he would or could be, I had trouble finding strength because I wasn't sure what remained behind.

I read the same books to him, sang the same songs to him at night, but now tears flowed and I had to turn my head away

PRISCILLA GILMAN

so he wouldn't see me crying. While we danced around to 'Here Comes the Sun' or 'Skip to My Lou', Benj as buoyant as ever, I'd clench my nails into my arm or bite the inside of my cheeks hard

"His unruffled indifference was, in fact, a symptom of the disorder"

to keep from breaking down, and would run to the bathroom afterward to sob, kneeling on the floor and running the water so he wouldn't hear me.

These precautions may have been unnecessary, as Benj seemed, as always, unusually insulated from my emotional state. Benj's obvious obliviousness to the larger situation, his living in his own world, which had once served as a balm and a solace, now enhanced the pathos of the situation. He seemed to have no understanding or awareness of the radical change in his parents' consciousness about him, and showed few indications that he sensed that anything at all had changed. They say that children always know when something is up, but I really don't think he did. And that his unruffled indifference was, in fact, a symptom of the disorder only heightened its poignancy for me. . .

* * *

It wasn't just my gravely ill father and my beleaguered stepmother from whom I kept news of our situation with Benj. I told no one but my mother, my sister, and my brother-in-law. There were professional reasons for my silence. I felt that I couldn't let Vassar know or they might not hire me; my being a young mother and pregnant with a second child were already strikes against me. And a child with a severe disability? Moreover, I was less than two months away from Yale's dissertation deadline and thought that if Yale folks and my friends knew, the flood of concern, sympathy, and advice would be distracting and overwhelming. So I told my junior faculty colleagues, my students, my dissertation advisers nothing of what was going on with Benj; I pushed ahead, completing and turning in my dissertation six weeks after the call from the nursery school in

New York. Richard told no one at all. I urged him to share some of what was happening with his two brothers, his aunts and uncles, his cousins, but he didn't until they heard hints via my mother almost a year later. And he urged me to tell as few people as possible, and out of respect for his wishes, I didn't even tell my dearest friends. On the one hand, his reluctance to share was due to his natural diffidence, his tendency to shun confidences and emotional intimacy. But on the other, his desire to keep things quiet stemmed from his uncertainty, an uncertainty I shared, about what there was *to* tell, a belief that there was no easy way to sum up Benj and our situation with him, that labels and capsule descriptions would lead to a reductive sense of who Benj was and a constriction of the possibilities for his life. We didn't want pity, we didn't want panic, we didn't want oversimplified explanations or unhelpful advice. We didn't want Benj exposed to 'the intruding sky'.

The genetics of developmental disorders had struck a blow to the heart of our mutual vision for our family. We'd wanted three or four children but now we wondered not only whether we should have more children but also at how great a risk the baby already growing inside me was for his own problems. The happy news that we were having another boy – 'It's nice to have brothers three years apart so they can be best friends and share a room, and then maybe we'll get a girl next time!' I'd written to my mother after the ultrasound in early January – now took on an ominous cast as we learned that hyperlexia and developmental disorders were vastly more common in boys.

Richard and I shared this worry about future children, but we also experienced the discovery of Benj's condition differently, in ways that separated us. Most obviously, Richard had never felt the lack, the disorientation that I had. He had never felt anything was really amiss in his bond with Benj. So now he was looking at that bond, and questioning his own sense of who Benj was and who he was. That Richard had brushed off my concerns by explaining Benj's oddities in relation to himself must have only intensified the horror for him when he realised there was actually something wrong. That every book, every Web site, every questionnaire emphasised that there was an inheritable quality to the disorder must have been acutely painful for Richard, though he never explicitly spoke of it.

And learning about the genetics simultaneously reassured me, about both Benj and Richard, and increased my anxiety. On the one hand, the similarities between Richard and Benj were comforting – Richard had been successful in good schools, had friends, gotten married, had children. In addition, they explained aspects of Richard's behaviour and helped me gain even more compassion for him. His brain worked in a different way, and he had done amazingly well with his life considering. But I also wondered: was Richard, too, fundamentally incapable of sustained intimacy and emotional exchange, of the kind of partnership I wanted in a marriage? Is that what I had been feeling all these years but not quite acknowledging? Would he never 'get over' his perfectionism, his reticence, because they were innate character traits? For so long, I'd chalked up Richard's difficulties completing work and his emotional withdrawal to grief over his parents' illnesses and deaths. I'd been overwhelmed with sympathy for him and a desire to give him the happy family life he had tragically lost. I'd believed that with my love and support, Richard would eventually complete his grieving for his parents and come into the world. But perhaps grief had little to do with it?

At the same time, I yearned to comfort this man I loved so very much and I felt powerless to do so. I knew Richard was afraid, angry, mournful, but he wouldn't let me know the contours of his fear, anger, grief. I couldn't get him to open up to me. I had always been able to reach him, always. But now I felt completely helpless. I'd always felt a powerful desire to make things right for the people dear to me, and I didn't know how to make it better for Richard; that was very hard for me. I, too, needed support and a chance to share my feelings and fears, but I didn't' want to overwhelm him with my own grief when he was so obviously suffering. So we never mourned the loss of our dream together. We never held each other and wept.

In 'Michael', a poem about a father's loss of his only son, which Richard and I had always especially loved, Wordsworth writes that

**. . . a child, more than all other gifts
That earth can offer to declining man,
Brings hope with it, and forward-looking thoughts.**

It was the loss of hope that so devastated me in those early days. 'Am I even allowed to have dreams and hopes and anticipation for his life?' I wondered. When did hope become fantasy or denial? And what risk was I taking if I allowed myself to hope and then those hopes weren't realised? I didn't want to set my son up to fail. I didn't want to make my goals for his progress too lofty or my dreams for his future impossible for him to fulfil. I didn't want to expect too much of him or ask him to give me what he never could.

These lines from Wordsworth's paean to childhood bliss, the 'Immortality Ode', kept running through my head:

**Whither is fled the visionary gleam?
Where is it now, the glory and the dream?**

My dream of Benj's happy life had disappeared.

**Questions, directions, warnings and advice,
Flowed in upon me from all sides.**
Prelude, III

There is nothing less romantic, literary, or lyrical than the language of pathology, diagnosis, symptom checklists. As I read through these checklists over and over again, I was struck by the harshness, the crudeness of the terminology. And once the evaluation process began, more and more distinctly unpoetic terms were added to the list, as the problems quickly grew in scope and seriousness.

Priscilla Gilman, *The Anti-Romantic Child: A Story of Unexpected Joy* (Harper USA, 2011)

LES MURRAY

LES MURRAY

O.K. Primavera Lips

The coral tree grows
in cowyards and old sties.
Thorny, tan in winter
it bears scarlet bracts,
red lipstick crescents.

Of Earth's most spoken word,
okay, just one suggested origin
is neither cheesy nor far-fetched:
Only Kissing. From saucy times.
Only kissing, Pa. O.K?

In fertile soil
coral trees pout lips
all over, before greening.
Ours didn't, until drugged
with superphosphate. Now
it grips itself with carmine nails

to the heights of wisteria
that cascades rain-mauve
down wonga vines and gum trees
and the Chinese tallow boughs
ticketed with new green.

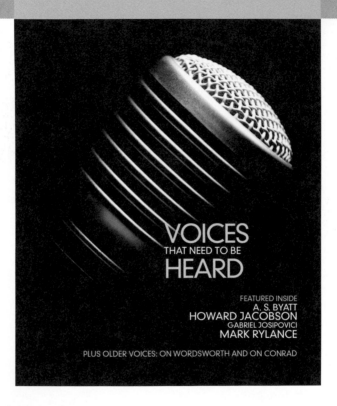

NEW WRITING / BOOK TALK / NEWS AND REVIEWS

No. 29

THE READER

VOICES
THAT NEED TO BE
HEARD

FEATURED INSIDE
A. S. BYATT
HOWARD JACOBSON
GABRIEL JOSIPOVICI
MARK RYLANCE

PLUS OLDER VOICES: ON WORDSWORTH AND ON CONRAD

I love *The Reader*. I love its pomp-free seriousness, its unpredictable mix of writers and subjects, its freedom from the corpsespeak of academic criticism and the demeaning triviality of culture-vulture journalism. When Dr Johnson rejoiced to concur with the common reader I assume him to have been thinking of just those to whom this reader unembarrassedly speaks.

Howard Jacobson

Selection from The Reader's Past

INTERVIEW

LIFE AFTER FIFTY

Sarah Coley talks to Jane Davis

SC: *Do you remember the start of* The Reader *magazine?*

JD: I remember talking it over in our kitchen at Bayfield Road. Phil had been in discussion for a long time with John Silkin at *Stand* magazine – Silkin wanted us to take over *Stand* – and then when those plans fell through we were all angry and disappointed, and I had got so fired up that I wanted to carry on and create our own magazine. I don't know who came up with the name, possibly Phil because he's good at thinking of names. We seriously considered calling it *The Abercromby Pig*, but it wouldn't have said what the magazine is in the same way that *The Reader* does. I don't think we ever had a plan as such. It was 'let's start this' and we didn't think about the future. We certainly didn't think of fifty issues, and now it seems the magazine just flowers each quarter like a lucky accident.

That's in contrast with The Reader Organisation, it seems to me. You always did have a plan or the germ of an idea for that. Almost every time we met you'd collar me with 'I think there can be this thing where people read for their own good and it's not academic; they're ordinary people'. It would be, you said, like Frank Alpine's moment with Helen, the girl he likes who wants him to read Tolstoy and Dostoevsky – he's got holes in his shoes, and she wants him to read these great books from the library. He says 'I'd rather read the truth' and she answers 'It is the truth'. We quoted that proudly on the back cover of the very first issue of the magazine, from Bernard Malamud's The Assistant.

I'm surprised to hear you say that I had the idea so early. It doesn't feel like that but maybe that's the difference between a plan and an impulse, or maybe *need* is the right word. I feel as if a lot of the beginning of The Reader Organisation happened by accident.

When I tell people the story of The Reader Organisation, I say it started with the magazine; we made the magazine but having *The Reader* was like having a beautiful pet, an intelligent working dog or a gorgeous shire horse that you can't actually *use* if you're not a farmer. It looks lovely in the field but it does nothing and it costs you money. So we started running Readers' Days to make some money. Do you remember the first one that Angie and I (Angela Macmillan, co-editor of the magazine) massively over-catered for? People were shovelling that spread into their handbags as they left at the end! But even so we made a thousand pounds out of that day by all of us working for no pay and by having free use of the University of Liverpool's Continuing Education building, which was kind of them. That funded the magazine for another span. But the people who came to those days were not the same people who came to our Continuing Education classes – well, many of them were the same, but there were different people too, people who would never come to the University because it would seem too remote or highbrow. We were reaching different people. Though I think for a long time when we were teaching Continuing Education classes – you, me, Angie – it set up an atmosphere where books were being read in a way that was not formal or academic. That way of taking books and poems for real, whether in our classes or at the Readers' Days, definitely did inform the magazine and it says so in the editorial of the first issue:

A loosely-woven yet very real community of readers has been born... brought together through what amounts (in all its various forms) to a shared hunger. This hunger may be hard to recognise, and even harder to satisfy when we read alone, without the experience and collaborative encouragement of others.

That fed into what I began to create in the Reader Organisation and in that sense I do think the magazine and the organisation grow from that same root. It's the same for readers and writers too. The first claim of the magazine was that we would have great and established writers alongside new beginners or unknowns, just side-by-side, and we've kept to that.

I read through everything recently – a small team of us did – to select highlights and there's a good example of that side-by-side quality in issue 24. There's Alan Davis talking about how as a boy he was fascinated by the night sky – he was set off by Patrick Moore's book Astronomy. *He went on to be a physicist but then later, disillusioned by the mechanistic nature of the work he was doing, he somehow discovered Ruskin. It's a story of two great transforming moments – too long unfortunately to re-print here, and you do need the whole of it. In the same issue, we had Patrick Moore writing about his early reading. We sent Alan's piece to him and I think that was good for both of them. What I love was that Patrick Moore had the whole universe as his subject but the book he had enjoyed as a boy was still at arm's length from the chair where he wrote that piece for us as an old man. Then there was Anne Stapleton's tremendous essay on birds. In this extract a power worker has knocked a nest to the ground by accident:*

He retrieves the world's error in his own two hands that know how to fix things. He puts the nest in a cardboard box and drives to work with them each day on the front seat of the truck, for the chicks must be fed every few hours. He says to the other men, 'Yep, I brought the kids today,' and they all laugh, embarrassed, but somehow glad. In between the brake jobs and oil changes and fan belt replacements, he feeds them. And they want to do their part in all of this: their every movement is directed toward the sky. Every minute they are looking up.

And then one day the first one dies, a fungus probably. And then one after another, one per day, as if by prior agreement with something pitiless and implacable above that does not want them, not even for a second. Their heads grow too heavy. They can no longer eat. One by one, they drop backwards out of time. Until the box is gone from the corner; no more need. Until the heavens are blank and smooth and clean of them as stone. But if you think this is a story about failure, you have only to look up from what you cannot keep.

There was also John Scrivener's great essay on Augustine, and Patrick McGuinness's fine 'Poet on His Work', both of which are represented in this issue. We called the issue 'Heavens'.

Looking at that issue now, that's a great title for my editorial, 'What's the Cosmic Point?' Ha ha!

That says a lot about what went into the magazine – not really knowing what it's talking about but keeping going and trying to work it out.

Yes. One of the things I liked best from the early years was Michael Macilwee's piece about boxing in issue 8. I had a hard job persuading the editorial board that it was potentially a great piece. I had to keep sending it back to Mick, getting him rewrite and rewrite... But when we did publish it, it was a marvellous piece and I was really proud to have brought that into publication:

'What are you going to do with your Ph.D?' has been a frequent question since I finished my thesis five years ago. I still work as a librarian, cataloguing and organising knowledge, but this is what Lucy Snowe would have called 'daily bread, hourly work, and a roof of shelter'. It beats packing biscuits, that's for sure, but it is a job, not a vocation. What to do, not with the qualification, but with my literary education, with the self that has been made by it, has been a bigger and more difficult question for me. Like Bellow's Dean Corde, I am sometimes troubled by the seeming uselessness of my education in the face of social realities. Indeed my biggest task has been the journey back to a very different social and cultural world. Here, largely amongst people for whom education, let alone literature, is irrelevant, I now struggle to utilise what I have learned.

Perhaps this is why, librarian by day, I am a boxing coach by night, rather than (say) an English teacher. The two types of work seem antithetical, the barbaric and humanising poles of our culture, yet there is a strong enough link between them for me. If reading literature involves the search for deeper meaning and under-

standing of self, seldom is that inner sense of self more exposed than in the act of fighting. Preparing boxers for combat involves much more than physical conditioning. Training involves the confrontation of the individual's fears, hopes and doubts. When you are working closely with the deeper reaches of somebody's psyche you can teach them much more than boxing. My aim is to instil in my boxers confidence and self-respect, two thing literature has given me, as well as discipline and hard work, a sense of fair play and respect for others, and a host of other values that will go towards creating better individuals and, I hope, a better community. Thirty years ago I was boxing to disguise my own emotional and moral sensitivity. Now I use the sport to inculcate just such sensitivity in others. My own life has been shaped and transformed by literature: boxing has become the form through which I hope to pass that on.

What would you change about the magazine given infinite resources?

One thing I'd like to do if I had more time is every issue have an interview with somebody, so this is a good start for a new start: life after fifty. In the past I used to interview people and I would always ask them about their reading life – did you read as a child, and so on – but now I'd like to find out mainly about their work and their life. With some of the people I want to talk to, books wouldn't be hugely appropriate. I don't think it matters about whether they are readers for the purposes of the interview. What I'm interested in now is the relation of people to their own creativity, that we all have the power to create our lives as well as inherit them. How did you come to be yourself, what's your story? That's what I'd like to ask people about.

The other thing I'd do if money was no object is that I would have someone to develop the marketing of the magazine. We've never paid any attention to any of that and it seems to me really ridiculous to have a lovely, beautiful, complex, well-made thing and not to be able to sell it or give it to people. Not enough people read the magazine. And that is 'the truth'.

Andrew McNeillie

Most lessons were a great mystery to me, for quite a long time – for far longer than might be considered 'normal' or average. I had miserable difficulties learning. Perhaps I had what are now classed as 'learning difficulties'. At any rate, by any standard, I took a painful age to learn to read. I found it a mystery and I'm not sure why. I found it hard to connect words with their sounds. I looked at them and they seemed like objects to me, opaque combinations from the alphabet, attractive but meaningless, except I knew that they generally meant what you saw in the picture above them. As long as there weren't too many things to choose from, that was fine. Otherwise they swam before my gaze like fish in a tank. My progress was so slow that my father, an impatient, hot-tempered man, took an interest in it. He was like Pa D on the home front, without the cane, but with far greater intensity of rage and I suppose far more pervasive and intimate and so crueller authority.

What did I have in my head, sawdust? – he'd rant furiously. I am sure this helped a great deal. But help or no, my progress through the Beacon Reader series was painful. Book One about the wretched farmer 'Old Lob' had me dug in for the long haul and not just down to Christmas. I was like those soldiers in their trenches in the Great War. The longer it went on, the worse it got. The worse it got, the longer it went on. In the process I suffered a kind of educational shell-shock. As for arithmetic, I couldn't even begin to spell it. Nothing seemed to add up, except blushing and burning unhappiness, and fear. (I'm still deeply challenged numerically.)

Words swam before my gaze. They were like the perch my father kept in a fish tank in the backyard. Their world was a

ANDREW
McNEILLIE

silent mouthing world. They couldn't say their letters either, but at least they were full of life and a different, an absorbing, mystery. I could stand and stare at them for half a morning at a time, feeding them earthworms and slaters and other grubs I found under stones, watching them dart and turn and vie with each other, bold, bright, green, dark barred, ruddy-finned, spiky hump-backs, darting over the gravel bed of the tank. The word for them: 'perch' – so odd after all, paradoxically sedentary, or more than five yards longer than any perch you saw. What sense is one to make of words? What not? The word is your oyster.

Then one winter the tank froze. The thaw came. The tank burst and the poor perch perished. Their silence now complete, they were like that 8lb pike my father caught and for half a day perhaps, but it seemed for ever, had hanging on a meat hook from the cistern in the disused outside lavatory. It seemed to me that I peeped in at that door a thousand times to hear what the pike had to say out of his big unfunny grin – it would have been a she in fact, as the bigger pike are – a dark, browny fish the way an old one is, scales now dulled, eye set matt, before being cut up into lengths and cutlets. Pike a good word for a stiff fish, like a pikestaff. The pike I would know on the end of my line were greenish, barred and spotted, with pale bellies, lean young fish, not monsters. Though they spoke volumes to me, hooked from the Bladnoch below Crouse Farm, the Bladnoch in which it was said there were pike big enough to take the leg off a drowning horse.

I am now more or less as literate as the next person. I have earned my living scribbling, one way, or another, for most of my adult life. It could also be said I have lived for language and the word, quite wildly, to my cost now, as well as to my gain if not to my profit, more than most people I know, following my muse. For this reason this miserable period in my education intrigues me. It intrigues me all the more that when at last I started reading, sometime again when I was eight, I did so as it were overnight, from nought to top speed. The thaw came and I was free at last.

I like to sound words with the eye. I don't say them audibly but say the words to myself as I read. Perhaps something in me wanted that then, or registered it even in such simple beginning phrases and sentences, and it got in the way of reading? Or perhaps it all was just delayed development of my wiring, complicated by attendant anxiety? Perhaps this preference for textured language is also a Welsh thing, a thing in my case derived from Welsh-in-English, partly alliterative, generally alien to English formations, with some residual trace about it that English is foreign in construction and sounding to the ear, if not in my case in vocabulary.

While I admire prose that's plain and even, simple, unaccented, measured, disinterested, I do love it to be deep and crisp and uneven, energetic and opinionated. I hate safety-first. I like sentences to go off at a tangent, or to have a little touch of opacity bred of thought's resistance to the expected, like jack-frost at the window, denying transparency. Such as now no one in our lost archipelago knows anything about. So frost-proof has our centrally-heated world become, so uninflected, so flat, so bland. I nearly wrote illiterate. How deprived you westerners and northerners are who have never woken to the ice fern-lands and frozen forests, the deep tundras, the Siberias in the window pane, as you take the temperature of the lino through your bare toes. Life should not be choked with cotton wool, as for the immortal wretched of the earth it is not. Stare at the word. What might it not do? What might you not do with it? Step up and speak. Spare not a thought for the chorus of doubt and disagreement or the disciples of perfection. All that will always look after itself.

Whatever the nature of my encounter with the word, the thing missing from the account is day-dreaming. All children are great daydreamers, their minds always at play. (What are you being?... What are you being? my two-and-a-half-year-old granddaughter demands excitedly to know of me, when I get down on all fours. A tiger, I decide, having up to that point thought I was being just myself.) For my part, when pushed and punished for my slowness, when struggling, I diluted my misery and confusion, and only made things worse, by deliberate day-dreaming. I threw the switch on my heart's ejector seat. My eyes skimmed off the page and my gaze turned inward in no time and I was away. The more I stared out the more I stared in. In fact day-dreaming has been my *modus operandi* ever since. Just so it invents this page with its illogical optimism and momentum, and air of necessity.

Brian Nellist

The first part of *To the Lighthouse* ends with Mrs Ramsey returning to her knitting and Mr Ramsey, that would-be Eminent Victorian, reading Scott. Charles Tansley, their intellectually arrogant house-guest, has declared 'People don't read Scott any more' and Mr Ramsey, who does, needs to confirm that what he admires is still alive on the page. He is a writer himself and fears that automatic dismissal by changes in intellectual priorities implied by 'people don't read'.

Mr Ramsey reads, with total absorption; 'His lips twitched. It filled him. It fortified him.' Egotist as he is, he has the generosity to find another life within his own while he reads:

This man's strength and sanity, his feeling for straightforward simple things, these fishermen, the poor old creature in Mucklebackit's cottage made him feel so vigorous, so relieved of something, that he felt roused and triumphant and could not choke back his tears.

Manifestly, Virginia Woolf's image of a Victorian man reading does not make him merely uncritical in his response: he needs a literature that will repay the absorbed attentiveness he gives it.

The answer to Tansley's taunt is *experto crede*, not 'Trust the professional', heaven forbid, but 'have faith in the man who's tried it' and that means because literature allows us all that privilege, ourselves reading. It is chapter 31 of *The Antiquary* that Mr Ramsey has turned to, the funeral of Stevie Mucklebackit. He has been a minor character in the novel, assistant to his fisherman father, son of a wild and 'masculine' mother, grandchild to the sublime and senile Elspeth. He has drowned while fishing in a storm and now lies in his coffin on his own bed. Jonathan Oldbuck, laird of Monkbams, the antiquary of the title, comes to the cottage to attend the burial. Mr Ramsey, always in competition with his own sons, with Virginia Woolf's truth of insight is made to read a passage about a father, unused to expressing his feelings, losing his eldest son:

> **At a little distance stood the father, whose rugged, weather-beaten countenance, shaded by his grizzled hair, had faced many a stormy night and night-like day. He was apparently revolving his loss in his mind, with that strong feeling of painful grief peculiar to harsh and rough characters, which almost breaks forth into hatred against the world, and all that remain in it, after the beloved object is withdrawn. The old man had made the most desperate efforts to save his son and had only been withheld by main force from renewing them at a moment when without the possibility of assisting the sufferer, he must himself have perished. All this apparently was boiling in his recollection. His glance was directed sidelong towards the coffin as to an object on which he could not steadfastly look, and yet from which he could not withdraw his eyes.**

How different from the writing of the novel in which Mr Ramsey himself appears this is and the difference lies partly in the apprehension of time. Virginia Woolf writes out of the sense of the momentary shifting of consciousness, with the page transcribing always the present, where in Scott it is like understanding afterwards, a scene visually recomposed in the tranquility of recollection. Twice Scott uses 'apparently' to remind us that we cannot actually pretend to become the old father himself and we are made to surmise his feelings by reference to an assumed wide experience of other seemingly stern characters resentful of being brought at last and too late to acknowledge their feelings. The tender words Mucklebackit needs the author to say for him are made in terms totally alive to his own vocabulary, 'beloved object'. The emotion is itself less apparent than hatred which is not quite that either, because what we really see is the 'boiling', the storm of inexpressible extremes tearing him apart. The 'almost' is like the 'sidelong' look by which he forces himself to see the coffin ('directed') without actually looking.

Scott wrote fast and it is the order in which the details occur in a paragraph which makes his points, as a fastidiously chosen diction would in a slower writer. For the watcher of that scene the father's face is a history of the storms he's suffered but for himself his mind is fixed on that single storm which is the reader's first clear knowledge in the novel of what has happened and his memory that he was prevented from going after Steenie one more time; cooler heads, gifted with Scott's own prudence, had made the decision that he was 'without the possibility of assisting the sufferer'. But Scott's own imprudence replies that wasn't a 'sufferer'; it was his son.

The German psychologist Theodor Lipps thought that our pleasure in any object primarily offered to our senses lay in our identification with it, in its reconstitution in our own experience, so that instead of two identities there is a single passionate blending, *einfühling*, which, according to OED, since around 1904 we have in English called 'empathy'. Scott requires of us not that aesthetic of intensity but a generous acknowledgement of permanent difference to which we are to bring heart and mind in understanding, the older idea of sympathy in fact. Sympathy makes rational objections, moral dissent, even though the text provides a basis for it, an irrelevance in the face of greater considerations: the 'facts' are more complex than any ideas we might have about them.

DAVID GERARD

(*The Reader* No.9, Autumn 2001)

To A Newborn

(For Imogen)

Gravely you look
Into each adult eye
And dazzle it with innocence. Your book
Is wider than the sky
Towards which you stretch
Exploring with fresh aim
Beyond your reach
Our world to clutch and claim.

Though puzzled now. We trust
Whatever may surround
You, love be yours that must
On home or foreign ground
Grant that in time you come
From which remembered shore
Happy or heedless, home,
Enfranchised and mature.

FROM AN INTERVIEW WITH DORIS LESSING

(*The Reader* No.17, Spring 2005)

Tom Sperlinger

I met Doris Lessing at her home in north London. Her agent had not replied to my first polite request for an interview, so I had written to Lessing herself about two of her books that had changed the way I thought: *The Fifth Child* and *Under My Skin*. She was wearing a blue silk shirt, with a collar that she unclasped. Her white hair framed a face that occasionally opened in laughter but which was for the most part watchful and contained. She is good at making her interviewer talk. Her answers often began 'Well' or 'You see' or, in a more direct turn-about from the question, 'No'. Her presence, in person as in her books, is formidable.

In *Under My Skin*, the first volume of her autobiography, Lessing wrote, 'I am trying to write this book honestly. But were I to write it aged eighty-five, how different would it be?' I began by asking her whether, ten years on, her perspective had changed. Would it be a different book now she is eighty-five?

Well, certainly you do get different emphases as you get older. The other thing that happens, you see, is that you remember things that you'd forgotten, so perspectives change a lot. The tone would be bound to be different because you get further and further away from events. This is the great gift of being old, you're very detached, all that *Sturm und Drang* or whatever it is disappears.

She has tried often in her fiction to capture the atmosphere of an earlier time. She noted how hard it is 'to convey the *feeling* of a time, later when it's gone, because it's always improbable.

It always is. Like the Cold War. It's impossible now, it sounds so lunatic.' She talked about the Spanish Civil War, and the socialist anger there had been at the policies of the British and French governments. She overheard herself: 'You see my voice is going back to the anger.'

The family left Persia (now Iran) when she was five and Lessing spent most of her childhood in Southern Rhodesia (now Zimbabwe). In her autobiography she questioned the selective nature of memory, asking how one can know whether what we remember is more important than what we forget. As we talked about this she noted that her younger brother remembered very little of their shared experiences:

How about my brother? We met after a gap of thirty years, because of politics. All this time, because we had this extraordinary childhood on the farm in Africa, I was thinking, 'Well, at least we've got that in common'. He remembered nothing before the age of eleven. I don't know why he switched off. He'd chosen to forget some pretty remarkable things. Another strange thing is that the house we were brought up in had in it a Persian rug [pointing to a rug on the floor], much better quality than these, a hanging like that [pointing to one on the wall behind me], which I picked up on a street market, brass like that [pointing to a lamp] and a table exactly like that. And I wasn't aware of doing it, that I was recreating. So we really are so patterned by things we've forgotten. Which is quite frightening. We're not as free as we think we are, let me tell you.

She asked me where I considered my home to be. I said that I had grown up in London but I was not sure I thought of it as home:

Join the club! I'm perfectly happy in Britain, but on the other hand I think I'm not at home anywhere except in a landscape that's disappeared. But that's the condition of so many people. This landscape that I can recreate in a minute in my mind, is not there. It's gone...

FROM SPORT AND LITERATURE

(The Reader No.34, Summer 2009)

Simon Barnes

never intended to become a sportswriter. I only made the move because I was sorely oppressed by an editor in the group of local newspapers in which I did my apprenticeship. His highly successful attempts to make my professional life a misery made me resolve to take the next vacancy in the group, no matter what it was. It turned out to be in sport, at the Redhill office in Surrey. My first thought was that I didn't want to write about sport. I wanted to write about something important.

But the oppressions were enough to make me apply for the job. I got it, as sole applicants often do, and at once I found myself translated into the domain of pickled gods and archetypes. I wasn't writing about anything important: only Redhill Football Club and their adventures in the Athenian League. Only the local cricket clubs. Only the local runners. Only the school sport and the hockey matches and all the rest of the routine trivia that makes up the sports pages of a local newspaper.

Nothing important, then. Only triumph. Only disaster. Only victory, only defeat. Only exultation, only crushing disappointment. Only hope, only despair. Only alliances, only betrayal. Only strife, struggle and dismay. Only fortune, cruel and implacable;

only fortune, smiling like a fool. Only vicissitude. Only joy.

And it gradually became clear to me that I was dealing with the stuff that novelists deal with. On the news beat, I had written about planning applications, council rows, road safety (must someone be killed before something is done about the Buckland bends?), local grouses (would you say it was hell living here?), liaising with the police, going to the magistrates' court, attending village halls and reporting fêtes worse than death.

It is not the local pettiness that matters here, let's be clear about that. It is the fact that a news gatherer never gets the whole story: only a glimpse. Everybody he writes about is involved in covering up and concealing. But an athlete in competition is emotionally stark naked in front of you: you have the whole story, the whole truth, and with it, a story that has its basis in some of the deepest things which humans touch. What mythology began, sport continues.

Sport is not news: it is literature in the raw. All that remains for the writer is the telling. When you watch the fastest man in the world complete his world record not running but dancing, you have a subject on your hands that no one could possibly better.

SIMON BARNES

© Richard Cannon

SHORT FAVOURITES

THE READER TAKES TO THE STAGE
Janet Suzman
Issue 31, Recollected Working Notes

Actors are always looking for things to rest their minds on. It's like crossing a rushing river – you look for the stones to put your feet on, so you can traverse this space which is in somebody else's mind. It's going *somewhere*, but you don't know where it's going.

THE READER GETS ANGRY
Gabriella Gruder-Poni
Issue 35, Scenes from a PGCE

When schools don't do their job, the importance of background is magnified: students from illiterate families are more likely to remain illiterate in a school that expects the minimum from them. Schools in the late nineteenth century were the catalyst for social mobility, but the schools in which I worked were devoted to nothing so much as social stasis.

THE READER IN TIME
Jeanette Winterson
Issue 44, Taking A Lifetime

In our lives things don't lie side-by-side chronologically. They lie side-by-side in terms of their emotional effect, their weight, and what they mean to us.

THE READER HAS TO HAVE IT BOTH WAYS
Sarah Coley
Issue 24, Not Misunderstanding

Early in her novel *Hester*, Mrs Oliphant quotes a French proverb, the *'defauts de ses qualités'*, the faults of your qualities, the negative behind the positive, the weakness of your strength. This must be one of the most sheerly intelligent statements ever to come out of France. Take a moment to try it out for yourself – whether you apply it to the people who oppose you (whose defects are fully apparent) or to those for whom you care (despite their weird mistakenness about many things).

THE READER SPEAKS FROM INSIDE AN ILLNESS
Richard Gwyn
Issue 37, Insomnia

I spot the power lead that connects my laptop to the mains, and it terminates in a rectangular white fixture, which I remove, thinking it might also function as a lighter, and I attempt to light it with the blue one, convinced that the only way to ignite a lighter is with another lighter. I can smell burning plastic, but because of the defect in my cognitive wiring am not immediately able to connect the smell with my own activity, until I realise that the melting fixture is burning my fingers. I am, at that moment, aware of myself as an alien presence, an utter anomaly, a man standing alone in his study having attempted, unsuccessfully, to set fire to a computer, or – which is the same thing – to his memory. The next day I find the blackened remains of the fixture hanging from my desk.

FROM INNER ANTHOLOGY

(*The Reader* No.14, Spring 2004)

Mark Crees

Earlier this year, I received a letter from a friend in which he told me that his mother had just died:

Please excuse my long silence but my mother passed away four months ago. All her life she memorised poems and occasionally recited them to me. And now they have vanished with her, every one of them. They were a part of my growing up.

When I phoned him up he said exactly the same thing, not only about the loss of his mother but of her many poems. 'I have been trying to remember the titles – the ones she told me. But I would know them if I heard them again.'

The letter has stuck in my mind because I wish I had met this woman. I am, at heart, a bit superstitious. I like to think that every time someone bothers to remember a poem they add to its value in some vital way, even if the words are kept entirely to themselves. But how many people now commit their favourite verses to memory?

It is not always an easy thing to do and it may seem a rather futile and time-consuming pastime. Why bother to remember a poem when you can simply photocopy it, download it or scribble it onto a scrap of paper? Why bother – for that matter – to remember *anything* these days? Laura and I went to a wedding in July and it was incredible how the congregation resembled a film crew: throughout the service people were fiddling about with their camcorders, microphones and digital cameras, turning what could have been a special memory into a cheap video. What chance do poems have in an age when the act of memory itself seems to count for so little?

And so, to help further the cause of what I call *The Inner Anthology*, this personal store of remembered poems, I have included here a few thoughts and pointers. *The Inner Anthology* is an invisible book that varies from editor to editor. It takes a lifetime to compile, it will never be finished or published, it uses no paper, cardboard bindings, string, glue or ink and it vanishes altogether at the moment of your death, but I still believe it is one of the most important books we take up. Surely the best way to know a poem is to commit it to memory.

A remembered poem is not like a remembered 'fact'

I say 'to know' a poem, but 'know' is the wrong word. 'Know' implies that something is finished with, mapped out, possessed. But I have come to realise that *The Inner Anthology* is less of a possession than a relationship, something which develops across time. When a poem is memorised you can take it everywhere; you can mull it over before you go to sleep, or you might say it to yourself in the supermarket or during a walk. And it is incredible how even the shortest poems can yield new shades and depths in different moments. I remember reciting Larkin's 'The Trees' on the top of a double decker bus one spring and for some reason I heard the solitude within Larkin's voice for the first time. On the bus the poem had the quality of an uttered thought held in place before the rest of the day's concerns took over. Perhaps this is because I was also alone at that moment and travelling to work (Larkin's poems are made for the solitary trudge to and from work, and yet you will only discover this if you have the thing in your head).

FROM FOUR HELPINGS OF MILTON

(*The Reader* No.24, Winter 2006)

Tom Gatti

In 'Four Helpings of Milton', Tom Gatti, Jane Shilling, Boyd Tonkin and Erica Wagner chose favourite passages from *Paradise Lost* and wrote a personal commentary. Tom Gatti starts in Book I with this description of Satan.

Him haply slumbering on the Norway foam
The pilot of some small night-foundered skiff,
Deeming some island, oft, as seamen tell,
With fixed anchor in his scaly rind
Moors by his side under the lea, while night
Invests the sea, and wished morn delays

Book I, lines 203-8

Reading *Paradise Lost* is often a bit like playing Blind Man's Bluff – you know where you are, but then you're spinning around, and now it is dark and you are dizzy and lost. You become aware of your arms hanging clumsily at your sides. You can hear your heart beat.

Even before his sight abandoned him in 1652, Milton was obsessed with the disorientating threat of darkness. Which is why, half-way through his description of Satan, lying like 'that sea-beast Leviathan' on the fiery ocean of Hell, he inserts a little story about a sailor, who, in the gloom, mistakes the monster for an island and moors his boat there for the night.

The story is traditional, and the moral conventional. But Milton's retelling does more than tell us that the devil is deceitful (surprise surprise): it captures intensely the sensation of being utterly, hopelessly lost. The words 'night' and 'foundered' are yoked together to compound their disorientating force. The 'Norway foam' is at once precisely located, and strangely insubstantial ('It must be a very solid Foam, that can support a sleeping Whale', wrote a rather literal-minded eighteenth-century scholar). The qualifying aside, 'as seamen tell', puts the little narrative in uncertain parentheses, and the haunting motions of the night and 'morn' wrap it in a misty haze.

Although Milton doesn't explicitly say as much, the sleepy mariner will be pulled silently under water before night relinquishes its siege. Which is close to what happens to Milton himself: later in the poem, looking for 'holy Light', his eyes 'roll in vain' and 'find no dawn'. Struggle as they might, for both poet and pilot, the light of the morning (physical or spiritual) is delayed – permanently.

Imagine it: you think you're on solid ground, but it is sinking. You reach to pull the blindfold off, but the darkness remains.

FROM AUGUSTINE'S *CONFESSIONS*

(*The Reader* No.24, Winter 2006)

John Scrivener

The *Confessions* are confessions in a double sense: they confess and acknowledge God as maker and author, and they confess a past of sin and estrangement from God. Perhaps the best-known quotation from Augustine is 'Grant me chastity and continence but not yet', which should be read in context:

> **But I was an unhappy young man, wretched as at the beginning of my adolescence when I prayed you for chastity and said: 'Grant me chastity and continence, but not yet'. I was afraid you might hear my prayer quickly, and that you might too rapidly heal me of the disease of lust which I preferred to satisfy rather than suppress.**

Augustine is quite straightforward about his earlier life, about his long-term mistress and the much-loved son, Adeodatus, she bore him. We cannot escape ourselves or our pasts, he seems to say, and conversion is not the introduction of new facts so much as a new way of apprehending the existing facts. Crucially it involves the recognition that 'Thou hast made us for thyself, and our hearts are restless till they rest in thee'. That 'rest' is ultimate, of course; conversion does not bring placidity but rather a fresh phase of enquiry on a newly-honest footing.

The *Confessions* are addressed to God – to 'you' (or 'thou'). I and Thou, the self and the other, are equally mysterious. 'I do not know whence I came into this mortal life... I do not know where I came from', 'Who am I and what am I?', 'I find my own self hard to grasp... but what is nearer to me than myself?' I may observe pleasure or jealousy or the desire for power in a baby, but I can only by inference suppose myself to have felt these, since 'I do not actually remember what I then did'; 'my infancy is long dead and I am alive'. On the other hand when I look into myself I find that the 'vast recesses, the hidden and unsearchable caverns, of memory' contain more than I can know or give account of:

Great is the power of memory, exceedingly great, O my God, a spreading limitless room within me. Who can reach its uttermost depth? Yet it is a faculty of my soul and belongs to my nature. In fact I cannot totally grasp all that I am. Thus the mind is not large enough to contain itself: but where can that part of it be which it does not contain? Is it outside itself and not within? How can it not contain itself? As this question struck me, I was overcome with wonder...

I become equally strange to myself when I contemplate my experience of time and successiveness. Here Augustine repeatedly uses the figure of a sentence in process of being uttered, or a song in process of being sung:

I am about to repeat a psalm that I know. Before I begin, my expectation is extended over the whole. But when I have begun, the verses from it which I take into the past become the object of my memory. The life of this act of mine is stretched two ways, into my memory because of the words I have already said and into my expectation because of those I am about to say. But my attention is on what is present: by that the future is transferred to become the past. As the action advances further and further, the shorter the expectation and the longer the memory, until all expectation is consumed,

the entire action is finished, and it has passed into the memory. What occurs in the psalm as a whole occurs in its particular portions and its individual syllables. The same is true of a longer action in which perhaps the psalm is a part. *It is also valid of the entire life of an individual person,* **where all the actions are parts of a whole, and of the total history of the sons of men where all human lives are but parts.**

A life while it is being lived is like an unfinished sentence or song; here too I am unable to grasp myself as a whole and run up against the sense of being radically incomplete. But the perplexities of successiveness and transience lead us to the thought of 'the eternal' in which 'nothing is transient, but the whole is present'. The reason has 'no hesitation in declaring that the unchangeable is preferable to the changeable, and that on this ground it can know the unchangeable, since, unless it could somehow know this, there would be no certainty in preferring it to the mutable. So in the flash of a trembling glance it attains to *that which is'*.

The experience of ourselves as radically contingent leads us to 'that which is', to Being itself – 'when I first came to know you, you raised me up to make me see that what I saw is Being, and that I who saw am not yet Being'; 'unless you were within me, I would have no being at all'. Though he is not manifest to himself, he is manifest to God: 'to thee therefore, O Lord, I am open, whatever I am'. But God is not in the same way open to us: 'How mysterious you are, dwelling on high in silence', you who are 'most hidden, yet most present'. The *hiddenness* of God from us is somehow correlative with our hiddenness from ourselves – 'For what I know of myself I know because you grant me light, and what I do not know of myself, I do not know until such time as my darkness becomes like noonday before your face'. Running through and behind all this are the great anticipatory New Testament passages: from St Paul ('For now we see through a glass darkly; but then face to face: now I know in part; but then shall I know even as also I am known'), and from St John ('It doth not yet appear what we shall be'). We have not yet been fully uttered. Or as the old spiritual says, 'Oh nobody knows who I am till the judgement morning'.

As some of the passages quoted may suggest, Augustine can be demanding reading: the analysis of time and of creation in the final three books is especially difficult – though intensely interesting. These books are omitted in some translations, but they are really integral to the problem of identity which runs through the *Confessions*, for whether I look within or without I am, Augustine suggests, perplexed by the same questions: Where do things come from? Where do I come from? How am I to understand my existence? Or existence generally? The mysteries of the self and of the cosmos are analogous – the one is a microcosm of the other, and the divine is inscribed in both.

We should not feel too worried if some of the anfractuosities of Augustine's thought leave us perplexed. This is thought on the way, thought in transit. We are still in process of being uttered, unfinished sentences, and Augustine deliberately, I think, reminds us that the reflections in the *Confessions* belong to a particular person in a particular place – 'what is to be said of me? A lizard catching flies or a spider eating them as they fall into his net still can hold me absorbed when I sit in my room'. How vividly this brings us into the room with him!

PATRICK McGUINNESS

ON 'FATHER AND SON'
(*The Reader* No.24, Winter 2006)

Patrick McGuinness

Father and Son

In memory of my father and in welcome to my son

In the wings there is one who waits to go on,
and another, his scene run, who waits to go.

I would like to think they met; if not here
then like crossed letters touching in the dark;

the blank page and the turned page,
the first and the last, shadows folding

over and across me, in whom they're bound.

'Father and Son' reprinted by permission of the poet from his collection *The Canals of Mars*, (Carcanet, 2004).

Father and Son' is a poem I am glad I wrote, though I would have preferred not to have to.

Most of what I write is impersonal; or rather, it seeks impersonality, which is different. I don't set out to express 'myself', but instead to express a feeling, a sensation, a thing or a place. This poem is not in my usual style, and it still feels, for all that it fits in the book and is fitting to its occasion, separate from me. It was also written after the rest of the collection, *The Canals of Mars*, in one go on the back of the last page of the book's proofs. It is the last poem, but its natural place was at the start of the book, a farewell and a welcome in one.

The biographical circumstances are simple: a few weeks after my father was diagnosed with terminal lung cancer, we found that my partner was expecting our first child. Well-meaning friends and family tried to help with talk of 'new life for old', of cycles of birth and death. I even tried out such thoughts myself, but it was no good. Replenishment of numbers *per se* has always seemed to me a pretty desperate sort of consolation. Besides, those who have dealt with slow death, death by illness, know that bereavement comes not in one go but in foretastes, in increments, all along the process – what you can never be ready for is the realisation that really you have been ready for it for quite some time. Another poem in the book, 'Secret Wars', is about exactly this: the war of attrition between the healthy and the sick, in which the healthy look past the sick into the illness itself and into the time that stretches on after they've gone. By a reciprocal but antagonistic process, the sick look into the healthy and see only the hypocrisy of health.

But I did have one hope, which seemed to me at the time realistic and optimistic in equal measure: that the new baby would arrive in time for its grandfather to see it. Since my book of poems was also going through the publishing process, it seemed also possible that it too might appear in time. Everything was in a sort of limbo. I remember writing worried letters to Carcanet checking on the scheduling, so I must have been constantly forming connections between the baby, my father and the book.

Why was I so desperate for this coherence? After all, what difference, really, would it make if they all did come together? Not much, but one is often powerless in the face of consolation, and especially of one's own consolatory mechanisms. They take over, even for someone like me, with no religion and no belief in afterlife, and who generally does not expect very much to cohere anyway. Anyway, I busied myself trying to express, through a poem, the connection between my father and my son. It was an increasingly desperate matter, since as the weeks passed it became more and more obvious that they would not encounter each other anywhere but in my own imagination.

I began making notes in my head for a poem based around exactly those ideas – the cycle, 'new life for old' and so on – none of which I believed in. I found it impossible to get away from cliché, and though I am not generally averse to clichés of emotion (often they're clichés because they are true, or felt as true), it dismayed me to keep writing them. I abandoned the poem and sent the book off. I remember being sad that I had not risen to the occasion.

In the end, my father died eight weeks before our son was born. No more limbo. Instead, grief and happiness, not mixed or mingled or fused but radically separate; the border between them so clear-cut that it was like leading two lives at once. Soon after Osian's birth, the book's first proofs arrived, and I thought I'd try again to write that elusive poem

The only idea I had kept from my various attempts was the familiar image of a stage, of a theatre, and of actors coming on and off. As it stood it too was a cliché, but I always knew that it was the wings and not the stage that interested me. The wings are limbo: a place where actors wait to come on and off, the populous shadowy margins that flank the more obvious goings-on of the stage. So I knew I wanted the wings.

This in itself was not much use, except that it caused me to realise for the first time how obsessed I am by these states and spaces of betweenness. Many of my poems are about border states or spaces between languages; situations of incomplete being or virtual encounters. Many of the poems seemed to possess a sense that things and people were most themselves when on the verge of disappearance, as if they gathered for one last totalising flash before they passed away. Really my interest in the wings was just an extension of that.

Posting a letter one day, one of the scores of letters I posted to announce Osian's birth, I thought about all the cards I had posted, from the same box, to announce my father's death a few weeks earlier. It seemed like a strange sort of thing to be doing, the one action covering two such different happenings, a sort of dark action-rhyme between birth and death. I thought of the French homonym 'naître' (to be born) and 'n'être' (not to be), in whose identical-sounding syllables the whole drama of being and non-being was played out: the natal and the terminal resolving themselves into … the *terminatal.* The word doesn't exist, but if it did you could imagine Beckett having fun with it.

From these rather grim and abstract reflections came a concrete image: my father and my son as letters falling down the dark interior of the same letterbox, touching the same sides, touching the same metal lip of the slot and meeting in the fleeting darkness of a sorting office: *crossed* letters. Now I had two elements: the stage and the page, and the suggestive idea of a crossing, a crossing over, of crossed purposes, and even the cross, an evocation of the religion I don't have. Through these I became able to envisage a poem about beginnings and ends that did not go down the usual path of commonplace.

I pondered that for a while, and how to connect them without making too much of a leap. Sitting at my desk correcting the proofs, the action of turning the pages became important, triggering the image of the pages as *wings*, and rendering allowable – by means of the wordplay on wings – the movement across from theatre to book, stage to page. I then thought of the way a bird in flight casts its shadow on the ground, and that gave me the two shadows crossing, and producing, from the non-meeting of bodies, a sort of shadow-meeting that was suitably unsentimental and yet symmetrical and fitting. This shadow-meeting answered an aesthetic need without pandering to an emotional one, and helped me to the state of mind in which I felt at last I could produce a poem. I felt sufficiently in control now, whereas before I'd found it hard not to slip into sadness and slush, but I was still inhabited by the sorrow that had made the poem necessary. It was a delicate balance – too much of one or the other and the whole thing would have gone again, or turned out badly.

The poem's final conceit, if that is the right word, then simply offered itself up: as the pages meet and are bound in the book's spine, so my father and son meet and are bound in me, who am now in my turn both father and son.

Yeats somewhere talks of the feeling he has finishing a poem being akin to shutting a perfectly fitting lid on a box. I don't think he means emotional closure – that would be impossible and probably not desirable – but rather aesthetic closure, the sense of having crafted your material, however limited or painful or ungiving, into an object that holds its shape under duress, and whose different pieces come together.

I jotted a full draft down, pretty much as it now stands give or take commas and semi-colons, on the last page of the book's proofs. My consolation, such as it is, is to have made the box from – and thus *against* – the nothingness that I know to be the case.

FROM IT'S THE THOUGHT THAT COUNTS

(*The Reader* No.31, Autumn 2008)

Howard Jacobson

Of all the pleasures of reading I rank this the highest – hearing a voice, speaking as it were directly to you – almost as a confidence – of something the writer has come to know for himself: come to know at a cost, or as a joy, but the knowledge of which, as he conveys it, feels indispensable to our humanity. This is the reading equivalent of having someone open his heart to you; and while there are many ways a writer might convey to you what he knows in his heart – and in a novel, particularly, the dramatic means are infinite – I believe that the intimate, naked, voice of indurated experience is what stays with us after all the paraphernalia of plot and what else has been forgotten. The measure of a good novel, for me, is that I close it much as the wedding guest hears out the Ancient Mariner – as 'One that hath been stunned, / And is of sense forlorn: / A sadder and a wiser man, / He rose the morrow morn'.

Of course, in any novel worthy of the name it is the entire dramatic apparatus that bears the burden of its seriousness, but nothing sets the seal on that seriousness, nothing measures consequences or sends the novel out beyond itself, so much as the voice in which, person to person and for time immemorial, we have shared experience and confided terrors. Seriousness has more than one accent; it need not always sound like the Book of Job or the Song of Solomon; I happen to like seriousness laced with laughter – but we know it for seriousness when it finds the words which seem to anticipate our final conversation, when we will talk of the things that last and the things that don't, and commiserate over our common fate.

In Johnson's *Rasselas*, Pekuah, a member of the Prince's party on his expedition to find happiness, falls into the hands of a wealthy and well-educated Arab – a man surrounded by a seraglio of attentive women, from whose company he cannot wait to escape. 'Whatever pleasures he might find' among the beauties, Pekuah surmises:

'they were not those of friendship or society... As they had no knowledge, their talk could take nothing from the tediousness of life; as they had no choice, their fondness, or appearance of fondness, excited in him neither pride nor gratitude... That which he gave, and they received as love, was only a careless distribution of superfluous time.'

On the face of it the language is unapologetically that of sermon – making a distinction between real and feigned affection, reminding the congregation of that which riches can never buy. But a phrase like 'the careless distribution of superfluous time' raises it to literature. There, as life hangs heavy on every word, we enter into the frustration and futility of the Arab's existence. In so far as he is judged, he is judged morally; in so far as he is understood, he is understood imaginatively – his life rendered as it feels to him.

Any reader who does not enjoy thinking morally will not get far with novels that matter.

I'm not such a fool as to suppose readers will ever again gather at the feet of a novelist – and if they do it's bound to be the wrong novelist. Nor do I know how, in a world where everyone's looking for seriousness, we can persuade them it's the seriousness to be found in novels – that voice, which is the voice of humanity itself, urging the mind to aftersight and foresight – they could really do with. I only know it is.

FROM MANUCAPTION

(The Reader No.9, Autumn 2001)

Raymond Tallis

And brother clasps the hand of brother
Marching to the Promised Land

The gesticulating hand talks to any and everyone. It is an inescapable consequence of its reliance on visibility that it should be visible to one and all. My wave may be directed to you, and you only, but everybody can see me waving. Indeed, I feel a little self-conscious as I wave you off; consequently, my waving becomes a bit of a performance. But the hand has other, more private, ways of communicating, mediated not by vision in a visible world common to all, but by touch. Only what is touched experiences the touch. Through touch, hand may speak directly, and exclusively, to hand. What speech, what new meanings may emerge in silence, when hand meets hand, when this master manipulator, explorer supreme, this peerless communicator, meets another like itself!

One takes another's hand. The dictionary that grasps everything has a word even for this: *manucaption*. This single action – a distal, fractional hug; a part-embracing part-embrace – encompasses a multitude of sins and good deeds, a thousand silent speeches, dozens of different modes of togetherness: the first step towards violation, the small change of companionship, the last comfort as the abyss opens.

Manucaption begins with the child holding its parent's hand: for safety, for comfort, for guidance, for nothing at all – other than for being unselfconsciously together with an adult who has not yet been compared or judged. (They are not types those adults but archetypes.) The little hand lies in the large one; the sky-rise parent beams down on the low-rise skipping child and all's right with the world. For a while, at any rate. Until the child wants to wander, to stray out of range, to be unseen. 'Take my hand!' – and the skipping and dancing drags on the parent's arm. Now, the hand is a tether: 'Do as you are told! Take my hand!'.

Soon, the parental hand is an embarrassment, a social as well as a physical encumbrance. The once innocent child, innocent of its innocence, becomes aware of its childish state and finds it to be cringingly infantile, like crying and wet pants. There are still, of course, moments of sorrow and terror, when the hand is grasped instinctively, for comfort. At the school gate, for example. Or at least for the first few years; though not in the years to come – not there above all, where the manucaptive fears the jeer: 'Mummy's child'.

And then the hands unclasp for ever. The parent, who sometimes felt tethered by the child she tethered – the child who went at her own pace and had an altitude problem, dragging down its sky-rise manucaptive to its own low-rise world – suddenly discovers herself to be free and, in her freedom, somewhat abandoned. The transparent, always visible child has become increasingly opaque and ever more intermittent in her visibility. The parent's emptied hand signifies a wider emptiness, a greater loss. The first age of manucaption ends with letting go.

RICHARD HILL

(*The Reader* No.3, Autumn 1998)

The Haunting

You cannot move for memories in here
Tripped up, nudged, shins barked in the dark
Against the sharp and unexpected corners
Of the other days
Smell, sounds, laughter
In the night they jostle, move around the house
In daytime visible
As photographs, as scraps of paper, names
The branches tapping on the window panes
Or the rain that turns the sky to slate
The wind that tries the gate
That knocks and breathes and runs away
Leaving me here
Not quite all alone,
Not quite sharing, not quite a home

FROM WHY READ MRS GASKELL TODAY

(*The Reader* No.17, Spring 2005)

Josie Billington

There is a moment very early in Mrs Gaskell's brilliant and woefully neglected late novel, *Sylvia's Lovers*, where the heroine – young, pretty, much-loved and admired – returns to her family at their cliff-farm home after a routine visit to neighbouring relatives:

> **They seemed as if they had never missed Sylvia: no more did her mother for that matter, for she was busy and absorbed in her afternoon dairy-work to all appearance. But Sylvia had noted the watching not three minutes before, and many a time in her after life, when no one cared much for her out-goings and in-comings, the straight upright figure of her mother, fronting the setting sun, but searching through its blinding rays for a sight of her child, rose up like a sudden-seen picture, the remembrance of which smote Sylvia to the heart with a sense of a lost blessing, not duly valued while possessed.**
>
> **'Well, feyther, and how's a' wi' you?' asked Sylvia, going to the side of his chair, and laying her hand on his shoulder.**

In every Mrs Gaskell novel there are moments like this where, seamlessly, in the very middle of its own unfolding ('and many a time in her after life...'), a sentence will slip narrative time and line, cross a threshold – at that little word 'and' – into a new level of meaning which does not belong to the narrated moment, nor even to the novel's story. The Sylvia for whose out-goings and in-comings no one much cares never features in the novel again. The evocation of that future into which the narrated moment passes as painful memory and a heart's chronic sense of loss, is as inconsequential as it is momentary – something 'sudden-seen' and apparently as suddenly forgotten. But it is at these moments which strictly do not belong anywhere – less moments, than vividly realised spaces or gaps in time – that this remote story of an eighteenth-century whaling community in Yorkshire will come suddenly up close and seem as familiar as any ordinary human story – as though in temporarily cancelling the narrated present of the story, these 'spaces', as I have called them, also help to collapse the distance between the conventionally separated present-times of writing and reading.

It is this loyalty at once to the continuities of time and to its implicit richness and density that makes Mrs Gaskell so good at depicting the intricacies of elbow-to-elbow intimacy, that of love, and especially that of families. If there is one single good reason for continuing to read Mrs Gaskell in the twenty-first century, it is that she makes the ordinary interesting, makes it matter, by quietly giving status to the kind of nebulous or residual life-stuff that is easily ignored or overlooked.

Carol Rumens

Once a week, my mother had a night off to go to the flicks with her favourite cousin, Auntie Dora, and this was his opportunity. He didn't tell me a completely new story each week, but invented a weekly 'series', each self-contained episode involving the same set of characters. These tales were not at all like the fairy stories and animal adventures I was used to. My father had found a compromise between the kind of thing he liked writing, I think, and the kind of thing he thought would amuse a child.

It was sit-com, really, set in an English village. There were no children or talking animals, just a few grown-ups who were, without exception, gratifyingly silly. They might have been stereotypes, but to me they were vividly real: the dim Policeman Plod, copied, I would later think, by Enid Blyton in her Mr Plod character in the *Noddy* books, a fussy spinster called Miss Prim, and a hilarious gluttonous vicar who belched in the middle of sermons. My father did the different voices and left plenty of room for audience participation. At the end, the spinster was always outraged, the policeman outwitted and the vicar preached his only sermon:

Dearly beloved brethren (belch) isn't it a sin
To eat raw potatoes and throw away the skin?
The skin feeds the pigs (belch) the pigs feed us.
Dearly beloved brethren, what an awful fuss! (BELCH).

My father and I chanted this together, always punctuating the sermon with the most revolting burps we could devise.

After I'd gone to sleep, he then sat down at the dining-table to write his own story or poem.

By the time my mother came home spinning on her high heels in imitation of Ginger Rogers or humming the 'Harry Lime' theme my father would usually have completed something. If he'd finished a story, and was happy with it, he would offer to read it to my mother. But if it was a poem he'd written, he simply tucked it in a drawer. He knew my mother hated that depressing sob-stuff, poetry.

'I told him to send them to the papers, but he never did. He didn't keep them. No. They disappeared. No idea what happened to them.' So my mother said, and I believe her: my father was a painfully modest man. He never showed me a single thing he wrote. Though he treated my little poems and stories kindly, it was as if he did not want to acknowledge any connection between my writerly ambition and his.

Early in January 2000, I made a pilgrimage. I went to the City of London, and found, in the shadow of Lloyd's totem-pole tower, and not far from the cracked humpty-dumpty of the 'gherkin', the short, twisty corridor of a road called Billeter Street. Here, I knew, was the site of Dock House, a grand Venetian-style building where my father had worked as a young shipping clerk. It had been bombed in the Blitz of 1941. I worked out its position by the numbering, and by the fact that the replacement building had in its stone porch a small carved anchor, which was the Dock House symbol. It seemed to suggest commemoration.

The new building turned out to be empty. There was nothing, no plate or plaque, to show its ownership. The company that owned it, like my father's company, must have gone bust.

I looked through a dusty window at workmen's ladders and bits of masonry: another renovation. The existence of a basement gym was advertised on the door: it wasn't open, though the sign looked fresh. There was no-one about.

My father's century had finished. He had died in 1979. He wasn't going to come even a little way into the twenty-first with my mother and me. I left my spray of freesias on the pavement outside the hollow building, pausing to imagine his daily footsteps there.

That night I dreamt I had somehow got into the gym. I passed rows of exercise machines, and went into a tiny back room. It was lined with shelves, tiny ones, like those designed for CDs. In each small compartment were crammed the paintings and drawings, the stories and poems, I'd produced as a child.

He had smuggled them into work and hidden them there. He had filled the dark pleats of the shelves with these brightly crayoned and painted little artefacts so as to keep them safe, and to show me that I was special to him. Perhaps I had entered his mind, and these were his memories?

He didn't like anything I wrote when I was older. He hated 'modern poetry' and by the time my first book was published he had dementia and was no longer able to read, let alone write. He only loved my child-poet self, which he hoped would never change.

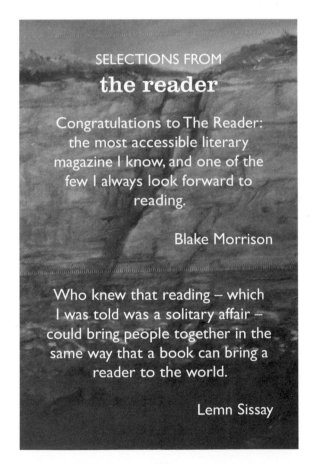

SELECTIONS FROM

the reader

Congratulations to The Reader: the most accessible literary magazine I know, and one of the few I always look forward to reading.

Blake Morrison

Who knew that reading – which I was told was a solitary affair – could bring people together in the same way that a book can bring a reader to the world.

Lemn Sissay

POETRY

THE OLD POEM

Brian Nellist

Henry Vaughan (1622–95)
Silex Scintillans **(1650), 'Peace'**

My soul, there is a country
   Far beyond the stars,
Where stands a winged sentry
   All skilful in the wars:
There, above noise and danger,
   Sweet Peace sits crown'd with smiles,
And One born in a manger
   Commands the beauteous files.
He is thy gracious Friend,
   And – O my soul, awake! –
Did in pure love descend
   To die here for thy sake.
If thou canst get but thither,
   There grows the flower of Peace,
The Rose that cannot wither,
   Thy fortress and thy ease.
Leave then thy foolish ranges;
   For none can thee secure
But One who never changes –
   Thy God, thy life, thy cure.

ON 'PEACE'

This edition of *The Reader* is full of golden 50s and here's another. In 1650 the Welsh poet Henry Vaughan published a collection of religious poems under a title which translated freely means 'Sparks from a flint'. He wrote as a King's man after the execution of Charles I, as a Christian whose church had been suppressed and, most intimately, as a brother whose sibling William had died the year before of wounds most probably sustained at Naseby when he was sixteen or seventeen. So the poem never mentions heaven but turns it into the tale ('there is a country') of a place that reverses all the sufferings he had experienced. It's what isn't said that matters here. Yes there is an angel sentry but he's not called 'victorious' or 'mighty' but 'skilful'. The soldiers are not 'irresistible' but 'beauteous files' and their general is no hardened campaigner but a baby from the manger who instead of being famous for the numbers he killed dies himself for the speaker. The crown itself is the smile on the face of peace. How to get there is the problem, this place of absolute security, 'Thy fortress and thy ease', and the bringing together of those two words should startle us. 'Leave then thy foolish ranges'; behind the lines is the acknowledgement that the world is indeed a dangerous and disastrous place where the only security lies in 'Thy God, thy life, thy cure'. That final word reminds us that Henry could not save his wounded young brother, though it was maybe tending him that led him to add MD to his name subsequently. To those who would say 'I don't believe in God and certainly not a heaven', I'd reply that it is the human significance that gives the poem its strength, the longing for a calm and serenity beyond all trouble. It is as Empson would say, yet another version of pastoral and, as Coleridge says, any belief entertained by people over a long period must, at the least, answer some deep need in the mind.

MEMOIR

WHERE I'M FROM, PART 2

David Constantine

was born more than a year before the War ended, but remember only scraps of its aftermath: the abandoned Camp and the bombsites, the air-raid shelters – the Lambs', for example, in which we played the secret games. I remember one brass cartridge in our shed, on the lefthand ledge as you went in; blackout material used for fancy dress; a bit of shrapnel in Uncle Norman's hand (by the base of his thumb); my father gardening in a khaki jacket. These few scraps. There was a gas-mask which I wore occasionally for fun. The shed door fell to violently against it, against its nose, and my eyes were full of tears of pain and shock.

Once I nearly put out my brother's eye with a sharp wooden bayonet fixed on a wooden rifle. I was chasing him round the shed. He must have turned, or I did, and we met. Escapes. I don't remember playing soldiers ever before or after that. (We played cowboys and indians, Robin Hood, cops and robbers, and on one occasion, gloriously, with long bamboo poles at the bottom of the garden, over trenches and piles of earth as it grew dark, King Arthur and his knights.) But we drew Lancaster bombers endlessly, flak coming up at them, bombs falling, air-battles, and had lead soldiers, ships, planes, tanks, and made balsa-wood models of Hurricanes and Spitfires. The comics were full of war stories. I conceived a horror of the Japanese, but knew nothing about Belsen or Auschwitz. On our bikes we imitated dogfights,

Where I'm From, Part 1 on p.33

with waterpistols fixed between the handlebars, riding fast, firing, veering away.

Altogether, outside events touched me very little. They make a timetable by the side of which my childhood must have passed; but just as into the garden, as I remember it, I crowd any number of events and details and there they co-exist, so into the whole period of childhood everything is drawn, into a suspension, disconnected, uncoupled from outside events. When these begin to be remembered with any fullness, clarity and political context, that is a marker of my childhood ending. The King died: I remember a boy called Jimmy Cohen (his black eyes, his big nose, his sardonic smile) skipping round the school playground singing in a demonic provocation: The King is dead! The King is dead! I remember the words Dien Bien Phu, the outside surface of the wireless set, silence in the dining room, the reporter's voice, and, from somewhere, an image of soldiers trailing along a trench. After that: Suez. But by then I was beginning to have political opinions formed by the Daily Express, and agreed with my friend John, who became a soldier, that the Americans had let us down. Christopher Craig, when he threw himself off a rooftop calling out his girlfriend's name, seemed to me heroic and romantic.

I now know something of what was happening in Britain and Europe and South-East Asia whilst I was growing up in Vestris Drive, and something (not so much) about the adult lives around me at that time; and I know that my childhood must be placed into those concentric circles; but it seems in my memory almost impervious to them. We were protected, the adults and their troubles backed away, they kept the world out as well as they could, for the first few years; but even without such efforts on his behalf a child inhabits a distinct cosmos in a sort of immunity, almost as though he were invisible, or as if, from his perspective, the adults were insubstantial shades on the perimeter. They share the earth, adults and children, they walk on the same ground; but if it were mapped from their two perspectives the look of even their commonest patch would be utterly unalike.

We had three parks. The nearest was Light Oaks, just behind the school, half way up Lancaster Road. It had a duck pond, swings, tennis courts, a putting green, a summer house and a long café under a glass roof. Buile Hill Park, that you could get to through the Camp, had a museum and a pitch and putt course. When we were small we could only go there with adults, because of the road to cross. Oakwood Park, at the very top of Lancaster Road, had an extraordinary wilderness in it, a steep-sided ravine along its northern edge. I spent an afternoon there with my friend John beating down the tall dead sticks of rosebay willowherb, all afternoon, as in a jungle, the violent occupation was entirely satisfying. In winter, when it snowed, we went sledging down the slopes of that ravine. The East Lancs Road began there, heading for Liverpool. Mostly we went to Light Oaks Park. On Sundays, all dressed up, we were sometimes obliged to go there as a family, for a walk and to have an ice cream or a glass of vimto. Having to behave well in the park was detestable. The park is a particularly clear example of the coterminousness and the utter difference of the child's and the adults' territories. The children move through the rhododendrons behind the flowerbeds on secret paths; get through the railings into the bushes around the duckpond; crouch there, spying. We annoyed the Park Keeper, and he pursued us through the undergrowth. Once he would have caught us but his cap was knocked off by a branch. We spent a lot of time trespassing, and not just in the parks; and tracking adults, spying on them, firing peas at them from clever bulky peaguns.

Not enough has been written about city parks – for example, about the large area of darkness they make after nightfall. To go in there with a girl is one thing, but to cut through on your own is quite another. The outside railings were taken away during the War, you could always get in, even when they put them back again there were always gaps. And it was queer pushing through a park from its nearest and most familiar entrance to its far side, and to come out there, not through a gate but over the wall, and not know quite where you were, the street was strange, the houses were different, of a different age and style. From Buile Hill Park, from the hill itself, you looked down over the inner Salford, the factories and the docks. Its walls were black, those of Light Oaks and Oakwood were blackened redbrick, we ran along them, over embedded plugs of iron where the railings had been sawn off.

We were always looking for something: caterpillars, frogspawn, conkers, cigarette packets, bonfire wood. The known world lit up every day in all its places that were best for the things being sought. Here again our own map had precedence, and we were bound to trespass. There was a good place for conkers in the first house on Lancaster Road. I kicked through the wet leaves, looking, nearer and nearer to the windows. It was most likely there would be conkers in the coach yard itself, where the property was most private. Looking down, for the conkers; continually looking up, for the man at the window. It was damp in there and dark, the trees dripped. If you got past you could climb over the high wooden gate into the Blind Home, or through Quarmbys' garden into Voltaire Avenue. The place had become some sort of club for men. That mixture of feelings – terror at being there and lust for the objects sought – was a familiar one. In brightness hardly anything exceeds a conker sprung out of its white skin, the feet kick through the dead leaves in a feeling way, to find the prickly green casings which have fallen and may be whole or split. The eyes of a child are exceptionally sharp when he is looking for conkers and when his kicking for them makes a noise and a man may appear and seize him for trespassing. Later when my passion was for geology and I had bought the drift map of Manchester and Salford, I was desperate to get access to those few places where the solid rock itself, a red sandstone totally blackened, outcropped; and had to trespass along the railway line near Eccles, to get it; and looking for fossils and bits of ore (nodules like a kidney) I slipped in at the gates of Mosley Common Colliery and rummaged through their tips. A geological map, in its beautiful colours washed over all the buildings and the roads, is a good image of how the child's world and the adults' coexist and are different. Even on a Sunday walk, obliged to walk sensibly on the usual streets, he can keep his eyes down, looking for cigarette packets. I loved the packets, the smell of tobacco left in them, the silver paper, the cleanness inside. Some were perfumed. And there were so many! Are there still? Dunhill, Capstan, Craven A, Woodbines, Senior Service... We cut the front off, what we wanted was the name and the picture, different sizes, fives, tens and twenties, fitting in the hand. Then it was something else. I watch the dossers mooching along on the look-out for dimps. The streets are full of adults in their private hells, muttering, suddenly raging, and every blind man or cripple faces the city at a queer angle, and all the drunks and lunatics, how slanted they are, and thousands more, in every city, who keep their obsessions secret behind closed faces but who are living oddly day after day. The streets stay more or less the same, the shops, the houses and the public buildings, and all the loneliness and idiocy dashes and shambles to and fro. Waking as a child in a particular obsession the map of the neighbourhood was at once lit up at every place where I could go and satisfy it.

The first family holiday we had was on the Lancashire Coast, near Presall, at a place called Bibby's Farm. I must have been four, Steve just born. We went by train to Fleetwood, then on the ferry to Knott End, then, I suppose, on foot, pushing the pram, carrying the luggage. Thereafter, for many years, we almost always went to Nefyn, on the Lleyn Peninsula. The longing for holidays to come was intenser than for any other occasion, like a physical weakness, a sickness. All year my mother put away tins of fruit and salmon in a suitcase on top of the wardrobe, so that we should have special things to eat during the week or fortnight when we were in another house. We went by train, from Manchester Exchange, we waved to Birch Grove as we hurtled past. Once, on the return, the train stopped unexpectedly at Eccles Station, and we trailed home with the suitcases from there. How strange the drive looked when we turned into it, and stranger still the garden after our absence, everything grown, the scented roses in an amazing profusion, the green trees.

Out of the first holiday, on the farm, I remember the terrifying size of the pig when it escaped from its sty, the belligerent geese, and the cows (I wouldn't go back from the beach to the farm through a field of them on my own). A couple of other adults were staying in the farmhouse. We called them Aunty Flo and Uncle Bert. Perhaps they owned a car and perhaps they took us in it to somewhere on the coast that has lodged in my mind ever since as a landscape pure of its kind, irreducible, so that if I ever came across it now the shock, the matching up, would shake me as though I had met one of my dead or on the street or in a bus or train suddenly faced a woman I had only dreamed about. It was salty grass, cut through with little channels of brackish water and pitted with pools, quite an expanse extending into the sands and the sea. Perhaps I liked it because I wondered how far you could proceed dryfooted across so many little veins of water, the place was like a puzzle for the eyes and for the feet. There were a few sheep, but nothing else, and it was very quiet. Also on that holiday – at least, I think it was on that first holiday – we came across a pool of fish and the pool was drying out in the sun. I thought of fish as creatures you could never catch or even come anywhere near. I had seen some far below me in the water when we took the Knott End ferry. Now we came through a gate into a field and there on the left was a pool full of writhing fish, a very shallow and crowded remnant of water, not much more than a puddle, and merely lying, as it seems to me now, on the hard dry clay of the ground. I had no desire to catch the fish, I didn't like to see them at everyone's mercy. Though they can't have been very large fish in such a place, they were not the littlest either, and in the mere dregs of a home left over in the sun of course they were far too big and far too many.

That salty coastal landscape and that pool of dying fish remain as images, outside any narrative, and I think it is correct to site them in the week we spent at Bibby's Farm. But the time is not important and I shouldn't mind if I was wrong. Many more such moments lodged in me when we began to go to Nefyn year after year, and they would be harder to place in time, and if by re-establishing contingent circumstances I could do it, and say which year and so how old I was, that would give me some satisfaction but not of an essential kind, since what affects me in these images or moments is their presence, their very presence, which is perhaps to say their freedom from particular time. In place they are precise, substantial, entirely particular, but often without a context, as though nowhere adjoined them; and in time very often they are freer still, and seem to exist in the sort of time where the memory and the imagination work in coexistence and past and future level out in presence.

How old was I when Aunty Alice and Uncle Norman took me to Stratford-on-Avon? I daresay I could find out, and if I were writing a biography of somebody else it is certain I should want to. I remember nothing of the trip, except this: a nest in a hedge on the way to Ann Hathaway's cottage, eggs blue as heaven, a path through the fields, sunniness. I love the image for its single completed self, and for its instantaneity, and have no wish to locate it more exactly by fitting to it any contingent details. I feel that to have seen a nest of skyblue eggs in that place of all places blesses me for ever.

Though the psyche develops it seems not to grow older; or it develops by a process which is not the same as growing older. I perceive myself in moments a year ago, or ten or twenty or sixty years ago, remember myself, and the self thus recalled is far more recognisably the self that is in me now than it is my own body. The moment I remember may have in it markers of my age, but my sense of that moment is not time-bound. I chopped wood at Trewernick, the Cornish house, did so for thirty years, almost every year, sometimes two or three times a year, behind the garage, under the cypress trees. There are numerous markers of time passing: the gales brought down more than half the trees, the neighbours died, their house was bought and sold, somebody new built an ugly bungalow, my son stands next to me, taller than I am. But I see myself surrounded by split logs in a place that changing circumstances have jostled but not overwhelmed, and my love of the wood, of the smell of it splitting, its shapes, its different responses to the axe, my pleasure in the character and the feel of it, all these compose the sense of myself as I am now and still, so that in that place, at that activity, I seem to be outside time, which for three decades was passing nevertheless. And when the place has gone, it continues in the psyche. Birch Grove has been reduced almost to nothing, there is no path any more through fields and allotments to Hope Church, but the connection between that old entrance and exit, as also between my here and now and the ground I walked on then, survives in me, it seems immediate, it seems not to be a connection back down a ladder of sixty years but to be instantaneous. Whatever lives at all is on one level.

I know it will not do to speak of an inner life, the psyche, developing in freedom from time, and an outer life in the world of time, because the intensest moments in the first, which endure and connect me instantly in what seems the very self, were made by an engagement with the outside world, which is subject to time: eggs hatch, the fish were dying. Altogether a vocabulary that splits us into body and spirit is misleading. In my memory and in my imagination, in my dreaming state and in my sense of connection across the level simultaneity of my life, there would be nothing of any liveliness and moment, nothing capable of quickening and inspiring me, had I not been bodily present – alert, attentive, sympathetic – when the chances were given me. And of course when the body dies that happy consciousness dies with it.

I began with the Gilda Brook and mentioned the stream at Nefyn that came down quickly off the mountain and got almost unspoilt into the sea. They are similar and different. Similar when I think of crouching over them, over either of them, sailing a boat or dragging a jamjar through the green weed after whatever creatures might inhabit there. For in that image of childhood it is the water under the eyes that matters, the clear water, sparkling and sunny, running from somewhere, it is true, and running on to somewhere else, but all I saw was what was there present under my eyes, where the launching boat was or the silver jamjar. The Gilda Brook never had any sense but that, and really where could it have come from and where could it have gone to of any beauty or significance in such flat and urban lands? But the stream at Nefyn – I never had a name for it – came down off a mountain and when I look up from the shallows where we sailed the boats (and by that I suppose I mean when I grew older, a year or two older, still not old) then where the stream came from was where I wanted to go, and did, out by the stream which was a gateway. The house we stayed in was very near the church, St Mary's, that had a galleon for a weather vane. I woke in the early mornings hearing the jackdaws. The stream came down past the church and just behind the house. I got up early to go for walks on my own. The mornings were fresh and sunny and the beginning of the walk was only a few yards away where the stream came in out of the fields past the church and behind the house. Where I began, where the gate was that let me in and out – into the fields and the zone of the mountain, out of the few streets and the habitations – there the stream widened and there we had sailed our boats. By the time I was old enough to go for walks on my own that place was already peculiarly blessed because of the hours I had spent there crouching low over the sparkling water launching boats in previous years.

CONNIE BENSLEY

POETRY

CONNIE BENSLEY

Aunt Maud and the Battle of Britain

It was all glitter and shine at Aunt Maud's,
where I'd been sent for safety.
First, the great marcasite ring
on the hand she held out to me (a present
she told me later, from her third pilot)

then the silver box of Balkan Sobranie
on the glass coffee table. I soon got used
to the satin shimmer of her peachy underwear –
often in evidence during the heat; and the shine
on the collar of her belligerent Jack Russell.

We lay in the garden and craned up at the bright sky
where tiny glinting Spitfires darted and swerved in battle,
sometimes exploding in a flash of orange
and spiralling down
into the green fields of Buckinghamshire.

Originally published in Connie Bensley, *Finding a Leg to Stand On: New and Selected Poems*, Bloodaxe Books (2012)

ESSAY

LETTER TO COLERIDGE

Anthony Rudolf

The person of William Cowper, in Brian Lynch's fine novel *The Winner of Sorrow*, serves as a manifold trope for Lynch's exploration of madness, desire, poetry and religion, all constructed as modalities of language and embodied in one suffering genius. I have not read widely in this poet of 'credit and renown', and it is time for me to explore my copy of his collected poems and take another look at Donald Davie's anthology *The Late Augustans* which reveals what Wordsworth ('as much the last poet of the eighteenth century as the first of the nineteenth') would have been reading, and ends with Cowper, whose death early in 1800 announced the end of the eighteenth century in more ways than one. That Cowper influenced Wordsworth and Coleridge is well known: in 'My First Acquaintance with Poets', Hazlitt reports Coleridge as saying that Cowper is the best modern poet. I am intrigued by the Coleridgean sound of 'The Castaway', Cowper's last poem, written in 1799, one year after the publication of *Lyrical Ballads*. This contained 'The Ancient Mariner' which Cowper could in theory have read, although Lynch has his doubts.

> **No voice divine the storm allay'd,**
> **No light propitious shone;**
> **When, snatched from all effectual aid,**

We perish'd, each alone:
But I beneath a rougher sea,
and whelm'd in deeper gulphs than he.

Dear Mr Coleridge,

'Was not writing poetry a secret transaction, a voice answering a voice?': Virginia Woolf in her novel, *Orlando*, a book my friend the poet Deryn-Rees Jones recommends to both of us. If you agree to come to dinner in Finchley, my friends (including Deryn, who will bring another poet, Michael Murphy) and I will listen closely to the music of your thought and attempt to engage with you.

I would not have the cheek to ask you about your 'delegated man' (hired in Bristol), your 'external conscience' as De Quincey [*Recollections of the Lakes and the Lake Poets*] describes the fellow responsible for preventing you from entering the apothecary's to buy opium, or about the person from Porlock, who may have been the local pharmacist.

Commissioned by the *Daily Telegraph*, my friend Victor Osborne invited me to join him in a walk following in your and Wordsworth's footsteps. We stayed at Alfoxton Park Hotel, once William's house, and visited your cottage at Nether Stowey, where you wrote one of your most beautiful poems, 'This Lime-Tree Bower my Prison'. We wandered through the garden of the cottage and imagined the route your friends Charles and Mary Lamb took that day while you stayed behind, having hurt your foot, and composed the poem.

Your biographer, my Cambridge contemporary Richard Holmes, includes the poem in his brilliant and original anthology of your work [*Selected Poems*] under the rubric of 'Conversation Poems'. These come immediately after 'Sonnets', and are followed by: 'Ballads', 'Hill Walking Poems', 'Asra Poems', 'Confessional Poems', 'Visionary Fragments' and 'Topical Poems'. Holmes's ambitious project 'is to transform Coleridge's reputation'.

And, indeed, how many people know your work beyond three or four anthology mainstays?

Holmes has done you proud, having made the necessary intellectual effort to honour your range, power and depth, your insatiable curiosity concerning philosophy, psychology and perception, concerning religion and mythology, and to present, in an enlightening framework of categories, the hard won rewards in more than a hundred poems, poems which now belong to the ages, that is, to your grateful readers in the 21st century. Your most famous poems find themselves in different groups where they take on new meaning in unexpected contexts and receive new gifts of understanding from the surprised and grateful reader.

Yours sincerely, Anthony Rudolf

PS I will invite H.J. Jackson if she is in England. You may want to discuss her fascinating book *Marginalia* in which you are one of the key figures. She writes that your 'marginalia in their desultory way dramatize the process of reflective reading'.

The attendant lord's trope of directly addressing the prince should be kept short. It is the kind of self-promotion (notwithstanding implied protestations of humility) intended to amuse the lord in question himself and even the reader, though for no longer than a paragraph-minute, if I may coin a unit. As if to warn me proleptically, De Quincey describes the sad reality of dinner parties at which Coleridge 'knew he was expected to talk, and exerted himself to meet the expectation'. The trouble was he was gloomy, withered and blighted (De Quincey's words) 'and passively resigned himself to the repeated misrepresentations of several of his hearers'. This 'regal mind' was 'threatened with overthrow... by the treachery of his own will and the conspiracy as it were of himself against himself', a sentence I heavily underlined thirty years ago and which still speaks volumes to all who in their own small way have experienced this treachery. 'The restless activity of Coleridge's mind in chasing abstract truths, and burying himself in the dark places of human speculation, seemed to me, in a great measure, an attempt to escape out of his own personal wretchedness'.

Let me open Holmes's 'Asra Poems' section, Asra being the anagram for his muse, Sara Hutchinson, 'that woman beyond utterance dear': 'Hence, viper thoughts, that coil around my mind, / Reality's dark dream!'. I have re-read 'Dejection; an Ode' for the *nth* time against its matrix poem nearly three times as long, namely 'A letter to Sara Hutchinson'. Holmes tells us that Coleridge showed this magnificent confessional poem to Wordsworth within two weeks of writing it. This is recorded in Dorothy's journal and, assuming she read the poem, one does wonder what she made of this record of another man with two women. It is a tribute to Coleridge's fundamental emotional honesty that section twelve, which can be read as self-deceiving existential 'bad faith', was written down at all: 'Be happy, and I need thee not in sight' and 'To all things I prefer the Permanent' etc. In his note to the later poem, Richard Holmes asks rhetorically which is the more moving work of art, 'the spontaneous outpouring to Asra or the profound meditation on imaginative renewal?' We have to answer the former, but sometimes we will want to read the more impersonal of the two works. 'Dejection' is a great poem: 'O Lady! we receive but what we give, / And in our life alone does nature live / Ours is her wedding garment, ours her shroud'. The matrix poem has 'Sara' instead of 'Lady' and *our* in italics, thus reinforcing the personal element. The gift of renewed understanding is ours to offer the shade of Coleridge. Poetry of this quality teaches us how to give and receive simultaneously, and its roots were nourished in the poet's 'shaping spirit of imagination' (the phrase survived from the earlier poem), that most profound of mental – intellectual and emotional – transactions, which sometimes emerges from the artist's inner battle to become the very embodiment of gift exchange between two special people: writer and reader.

From *Silent Conversations: A Reader's Life*, published by Seagull Books/ Chicago University Press in summer 2013

WANTED!

CAN YOU HELP SOLVE THE
CALDERSTONES MYSTERY?

WHY WAS THE PAINTING DESTROYED?
WHO STOLE THE MISSING PIECE?
LET US KNOW WITH STORIES AND PICTURES!

REWARD

$ BOOKS AND TREATS $

WELCOME TO CALDERSTONES:

WE WILL BE PAINTING SOON!

ON BALANCE

Casi Dylan

Having moved house last week, I have recently come face-to-face with the dust-covered archive of my attempts at self-improvement. Behind the wardrobe, the violin and music books. There's the skipping rope, the dumbbells. And – ah yes! – the *Teach Yourself Latin Grammar*, spine uncreased. I carried them with me when I moved down two flights of tenement steps and up two more flights of tenement steps at the far side of the city. And here they are, in several unpacked boxes, visions of a different, better, self. Folk-musical me. Grammatical me. That me who takes regular exercise, eats a balanced diet.

Personally, professionally, in the space between them, this balance seems an elusive goal. Much of my work at The Reader Organisation has been concerned with raising future practitioners to awareness of the crucial balancing acts of shared reading practice. Any practitioner will tell you that it takes a huge amount of energy to balance even the most basic requirements of getting a group to work. I'm thinking of Jenny and Bill in my first group in Salford. Jenny was a middle-aged black woman with multiple learning difficulties, whose medication made her speech slow and eyelids heavy. She struggled to follow the flow of the writing and the conversations that followed, and was largely silent unless directly prompted to share her thoughts. Bill – who always sat at the opposite side of the table – was a highly-intelligent, unemployed local man just turning fifty. He was often on edge, and his anxiety came out in his compulsion to show us how well-read he was, speaking at a level and a pace that deliberately left the rest of us, and the book we were sharing, behind. Catering for both Jenny and Bill within the same group was difficult, not least when it came to choosing the materials we would read together. For our first novel, I chose *Skellig* by David Almond. Bill wasn't keen to begin with, but Jenny was intrigued by the promised mystery of the story and she liked the cover. As we read through week by week, I noticed how both of them found their place – a new place – in relation to the story. Bill, despite initial complaints about reading a 'kid's book', became interested in the connections that he found in it to William Blake. We closed one session with 'A Poison Tree', and the following week Bill appeared with his bashed leather briefcase crammed with photocopies of poems by Blake. We read them together after the group and shared our favourites. Bill loved it.

It was the change in his attitude to Jenny that was most moving. Even though she struggled to participate in the conversation, Jenny was always the first to volunteer when the offer came to read aloud. This had to be handled carefully, as her reading was very slow: a single paragraph could take a full five minutes to read, and this accompanied all the while by Bill shifting awkwardly in his chair, huffing and eye-rolling. I knew that I needed to hold this space for Jenny, that this was what she had to offer us, and so every week as Bill continued to huff Jenny would continue to slowly read. I would step in to stop her and thank her when the time felt right. She read:

He was lying there in the darkness behind the tea chests, in the dust and dirt. It was as if he'd been there forever. He was filthy and pale and dried out and I thought he was dead. I couldn't have been more wrong. I'd soon begin to see the truth about him, that there'd never been another creature like him in the world.

And slowly, over time, Bill would fidget less in his chair, and became quieter, calmer. He began to pay attention to the book as the slowness of Jenny's reading demanded of him. I do not think he ever said 'well read!' or 'thank you' – I did, and so did others in the group – but I knew that those five minutes when Jenny read allowed Bill to relax and find a space that otherwise he would not have been able to give himself any other time of that day.

I am not saying that Jenny and Bill 'met in the middle', or found a happy balance 'in the middle ground' but I know they met in the book, and that they met there through a version of me, that applied personality, using the literature to hold a space open for them. Neither of these – the literature, the personality – is a particularly balanced thing. In fact, it is often quite the opposite, and all the better for that: both literature and personality bring with them an excess of focused belief, of attention to detail, of particulars serving larger wholes. We are lucky as literary thinkers and doers that we need not approach our work within the confines of either-or; our skills are based on the awareness of seeming contradictions co-existing:

> **ONE'S-SELF I sing—a simple, separate Person;**
> **Yet utter the word Democratic, the word En-masse.**

It's the self-confidence of Whitman's song that I love here. Partly, I think that the role of Literary Learning is to nurture and maintain such whole-hearted belief. We describe our work as a bringing about a Reading Revolution, of re-positioning literature at the heart of our lives. Our health-services; our education. This will not happen if we commit ourselves to a balanced approach. Perhaps the good that shared reading can do relies in part on every practitioner understanding the benefits of the productive *im*balance which working with literature can serve: our commitment to breakthroughs as much as break-evens. As dangerous as, say, a Gerard Manley Hopkins sonnet, or Tolstoy's *The Death of Ivan Ilych* may be, I know that they are no more dangerous than the version of me which creeps towards steady, deadening security at the expense of something more alive. I am more likely to forget my commitment to serve the lively excellence of the writing than I am to forget kindness towards the group members, or respect, or care. It's this stunting maintenance that frightens me, as in this poem by Sir Philip Sidney:

> **IF I could think how these my thoughts to leave;**
> **Or thinking still my thoughts might have good end:**

If rebel sense would reason's law receive;
Or reason foiled would not in vain contend:
Then might I think what thoughts were best to think;
Then might I wisely swim, or gladly sink.

If either you would change your cruel heart;
Or cruel still, time did your beauty stain;
If from my soul, this love would once depart;
Or for my love, some love I might obtain:
Then might I hope a change or ease of mind;
By your good help, or in myself to find.

But since my thoughts in thinking still are spent,
With reason's strife, by sense's overthrow;
You fairer still, and still more cruel bent;
I loving still a love, that loveth none:
I yield and strive; I kiss and curse the pain,
Thought, reason, sense, time, you and I maintain.

The poem adds up beautifully, tragically. All elements are balanced and stuck, summarised, comma by comma, kept separate in that final line. What is left to 'maintain' at the end is not the love which is so desperately sought, but the framework which the poem has created for itself to rationalise this strength of feeling. 'Then might I think', 'Then might I hope', but the tools at his disposal are insufficient for the necessary movement to get to that 'then'. Every time I read this it feels timely; it re-wakes me to the necessity of breaking through maintenance and onto movement. This has never been more relevant at The Reader Organisation than now, a time when we have appointed our first Quality Practice Manager, and are working on a framework to measure and support high-quality shared reading practice. There must be movement in these scales of quality by which we measure ourselves.

And when in search of movement, turn to Lawrence. Read him now, in *Women in Love*, when Rupert Birkin, school-inspector, comes to visit Ursula Brangwen's classroom, where she is 'leading the children by questions to understand the structure and the meaning of catkins':

This day had gone by like so many more, in an activity that was like a trance. At the end here was a little haste, to finish what was in hand. She was pressing the children with questions, so that they should know all they were to know, by the time the gong went. She stood in shadow in front of the class, with catkins in her hand, and she leaned towards the children, absorbed in the passion of instruction.

She heard, but did not notice the click of the door. Suddenly she started. She saw, in the shaft of ruddy, copper-coloured light near her, the face of a man. It was gleaming like fire, watching her, waiting for her to be aware. It startled her terribly. She thought she was going to faint. All her suppressed, subconscious fear sprang into being, with anguish.

'Did I startle you?' said Birkin, shaking hands with her. 'I thought you had heard me come in.'

'No,' she faltered, scarcely able to speak. He laughed, saying he was sorry. She wondered why it amused him.

'It is so dark,' he said. 'Shall we have the light?'

And moving aside, he switched on the strong electric lights. The class-room was distinct and hard, a strange place after the soft dim magic that filled it before he came. Birkin turned curiously to look at Ursula. Her eyes were round and wondering, bewildered, her mouth quivered slightly. She looked like one who is suddenly wakened. There was a living, tender beauty, like a tender light of dawn shining from her face. He looked at her with a new pleasure, feeling gay in his heart, irresponsible.

Birkin turns on the light in a room which Ursula had not noticed had become dark. I recently read this passage with a group who resented him for this. 'That room is so cosy before he comes in, with Ursula, "absorbed in the passion of instruction" He ruins it.' 'And he is so bossy', says Maggie, as we read on to when Birkin advises Ursula to adapt her teaching method:

'Give them some crayons, won't you?' he said, 'so that they can make the gynaecious flowers red, and the androgynous yellow. I'd chalk them in plain, chalk in nothing else, merely the red and the yellow. Outline scarcely matters in this case. There is just the one fact to emphasise.'

'I haven't any crayons,' said Ursula.

'There will be some somewhere—red and yellow, that's all you want.'

Ursula sent out a boy on a quest.

'It will make the books untidy,' she said to Birkin, flushing deeply.

'Not very,' he said. 'You must mark in these things obviously. It's the fact you want to emphasise, not the subjective impression to record. What's the fact?— red little spiky stigmas of the female flower, dangling yellow male catkin, yellow pollen flying from one to the other. Make a pictorial record of the fact, as a child does when drawing a face—two eyes, one nose, mouth with teeth—so—' And he drew a figure on the blackboard.

Bossy? Perhaps. Views will vary on this. Balanced? Probably not. Useful? Necessary? I think so. It is never an easy thing when someone bears witness to how you can sometimes slip into 'an activity that was like a trance', or questions what you understand to be 'facts'. I'm fascinated by Birkin's use of that word here, that 'merely the red and the yellow' is enough to capture those catkins. By 'fact' I think I understand him to mean 'essence', and that as a teacher it's Ursula's role to see and reveal what is essential in her subject, as that new light reveals to Birkin something essential in Ursula herself: 'a living, tender beauty, like a tender light of dawn shining from her face.'

Our renewed drive towards quality practice allows the opportunity to revisit Literary Learning's offer, to reassess what we mean by a truly literary education. To blow off the dust and get back to what's essential. It doesn't matter if it's 'untidy'.

THE READING REVOLUTION

TEN STORIES

CATHEDRAL

Alexis McNay

'The men who began their life's work on them, they never lived to see the completion of their work. In that wise, bub, they're no different from the rest of us, right?'

young man appears at the door – a boy, really, who looks like he should be kicking through leaves. He's rangy, with a delicate complexion, kind eyes and a slightly unkempt look. Can he join in? Yes, of course. We're strangers, and we're quickly reading together, and this seems to make him a bit giddy. He's not used to this kind of thing, and he really struggles anyway to focus, to concentrate, to follow; a wandering gaze echoing a mind that sometimes interrupts the story or discussion to ask the time or the make of my watch. It's hard to know whether the story is registering at all, but he wants to talk, to come out with things. After each break as I retrace the story and resume reading, I have garnered another little intimacy; his family has a history of mental illness; he believes in ghosts. He talks casually about this personal stuff, and one could begin to believe him thick-skinned enough. The biggest revelation he saves until toward the end of the session. We've finished the story, and he rolls up the sleeves of his sweatshirt, again, matter-of-factly, to reveal cuts the length of his fore-arms. The moment empties of everything except an odd tranquility. I sit here, now, wondering why I felt this. All I can say is that it felt like the moment had something to do with trust and opportunity. A couple of abstracts, but important ones. I'm calm, awaiting my response. The tutor accompanying me is perhaps as conscious as me of the delicacy of the moment, but he either panics or has his own formula to hand. 'Don't think you're going to get any sympathy', he says, 'you know what that is, don't you? It's just stupid.' The boy doesn't react, but the moment has changed. I don't know the right thing, but I hear myself saying, 'it's a shame... they're nice arms.'

* * *

Last week's group would have loved *Cathedral* by Raymond Carver, but none of last week's group are here. One has been shipped-out, another transferred to another wing, another is 'on laundry'. 'The priest' has been moved to a different prison after, if the prison officer's account is accurate, 'getting too friendly with some of the young lads'. In a rush this morning, I didn't bring an alternative story. I have only two men in the group, both new, the young man and an old man, both of whom have found themselves here by chance. Carver's wonderful story – no plot, unstable first-person narrative voice, metaphor and epiphany of faith and vision complicated by the characters' smoking of cannabis – isn't perhaps the one I would have brought in hindsight. I've been here before, though, in front of a group with a text that feels dangerous because it's a bit difficult, different or weird, and there's exhilaration on the edge of the abyss. If I take the plunge, it's not just because I like to fly by the seat of my pants, but because I know that some of the best shared reading groups that I've been part of have been with quirky-toned texts that have presented some challenge to easy alignment or comprehension. I've sat and read for ten minutes aware of a circle of quizzical looks, uncertain mumbles and awkward giggles, all suggesting the possibility of detachment if not unrest, and then gradually people lean in, interested in the novelty of the voice, taken in by the revelation that good books can do this kind of thing, intrigued by their own interest. I like Kafka's ice axe, but I prefer Eisenstein's slightly more gentle phrase – challenging 'the inertia of perception' – for thinking about the potential for literature to present different views, or the same views from different angles, in order to challenge or test the (hard) wiring of our minds. This is great when it happens and more of this later, but, to get back to the group in hand, I have to say that *Cathedral* bombs. That is to say that whatever pleasure or appreciation might have been happening as we read the story did not manifest itself in comments and/or discussion explicitly traceable to that story. I came away thinking that the story – or rather my choice of it, *pace* Carver – had failed. Yet I also thought the session was, particularly in relation to the young man, a success, and that something to do with literature has happened despite the apparent surface failure of the literary.

Get into Reading groups happen at the nexus of many needs, but I don't want to talk here about the enhanced opportunity for meaningful social interaction or the warm offer we make of acceptance and inclusion, though I don't think the importance of these can be overstated and I do think they were in play during this session. What has bothered me is trying to explain what I feel; that our core resources, reading and literature, are important even – if not *especially* – in a session where the men attending don't seem able or willing to engage with the literature in many ways that in a traditional reading group would be fundamental to its appreciation. In the case of *Cathedral*, I had no evidence that the men in the group had a firm grasp of what was going on, either on the surface level of narrative or on the deeper level of what the story's *about*. I didn't feel them engage with the characters. It was hard, then, to establish any discussion on an emotional/ intellectual level with the story or its themes. But that the young man enjoyed the session, of which I am sure, had much to do with reading.

There are things to do with reading aloud. This, for example, happens all the time: a man will appear reluctant to read, will say 'I'm not very good' or even 'I can't read', but will then find courage in an atmosphere sufficiently relaxed and company vocally encouraging to take the plunge, and they will do pretty well, and really enjoy it, and soon want another go. It represents a significant transformation of self-esteem, confidence and self-awareness before your eyes. This happens to the young man, who reads three times in short bursts, saying that 'the letters start swimming' after a while. He visibly enjoys being involved in reading.

There is something perhaps more significant in being read to, beyond the comforting and relaxing effects that are often cited by the men themselves in their feedback. I am often aware of new men in the group watching me as I read. It's hard to gauge

" It is an intimate act, throwing your voice, attached to the emotional stuff of literature and yourself both, out into a room"

what is behind this look – some aggregate of curiosity, surprise, interest, incredulity, bafflement – but I think this is the point; it seems generally positive and appreciative because they respect the chance I'm taking. I would speculate that most of these men are unused to the kind of intimacy implied by being read to by another man, and that they read it as an act of trust on my part to do so without knowing what they think of it all. After all, it is an intimate act, throwing your voice, attached to the emotional stuff of literature and yourself both, out into a room. It's also an act of generosity, when you don't expect anything in return, a little investment in we don't know what. This makes it a rare communicative transaction in an institutional setting. When the young man shows me the harm he's done to himself at the end of the session, maybe he's just showing off, trying to get attention. Maybe the tutor's no nonsense approach is valid. But

I can't help thinking that the display is an offering of trust in exchange for my reading to him, listening to him read.

That's the reading, but what of the literature, the words on the page? Is Carver more valuable than the sports page? It's hard to say, as I say, given the lack of response to the story in terms of discussion generated. But it seemed to me the young man did respond to and enjoy *Cathedral*, judging by his mood in the room, and the fact that he listened throughout, even if he would give a pretty patchy synopsis if asked what it was about. He certainly wouldn't say it was about how kooky language can trigger pleasurable and novel reactions, yet, if nothing else happened, this did, modestly. Therefore, when the narrator describes one of the blind man's little idiosyncrasies – 'The blind man brought his hand up under his beard. He lifted his beard slowly and let it drop.' – and I see an amused smile flash across the young man's face, I know that language in its own right has done something. I look up as I read and, catching the young man's eye, grin with him. We share a joke, though neither of us knows quite what the other is finding funny, or, indeed, what this isolated detail is telling us about the character it describes. I suppose the young man feels what I do; swept along with this narrator, at once so cock-sure and so vulnerable, willing to take us into his confidence, inviting us to see things from his point of view and to sense the fallibility of that view. I've used this story here, before, and had a group much more forthcoming about what's going on in that gap, really run the gamut of themes. For all my gentle prodding and probing, this doesn't happen on this occasion, which, whatever the reason, is fine. We talk about other stuff, the tangents of which may have had a logic connected to the reading for the young man. To be asked, though, 'how do you feel about...', 'what do you make of...', this seems novel and pleasurable enough in itself to him, even if he's uncertain in reply.

There's a kind of commonplace recognition available to young men like this in the prison, from staff and other inmates, which is willing to acknowledge that these boys are 'bad', that they are streetwise, that they have nous for banter and the ways of this limited world – in short, that constantly reiterates where they've come from. There is not enough allowance for where they might go.

This young man, as many others like him do, flits in and out of the group over the next few weeks, and then vanishes. Whenever I do see him, he has a smile on his face. Some of the other men in the group over the next few weeks get impatient with him, understandably – they are more focused readers and his tendency remains to interrupt, fidget and derail discussion. There's a job just to reconcile these different needs when you see that it *is* important for him, where others see just a timewaster, but that's another story. When he's gone I wonder, as I do with many others like him, though it may be pointless and I can only speculate, whether he took anything of it with him. For me, there's that image of him rolling up his sleeves. I can only speculate, and I won't. If it was just that session, just that day, though, I'm confident that it was worthwhile. I'm confident that reading was worthwhile, not on this occasion for anything that might be called literary thought or discussion, but perhaps, to allow T.S. Eliot a beautiful encapsulation, as 'music heard so deeply / That it is not heard at all, but you are the music / While the music lasts.'

'Cathedral' is part of a five-part series, 'Ten Stories'. Each piece explores a particular session in which the story that is read reflects back on – and tells a story about – the work that we do.

YOUR REGULARS

RETURN OF THE SPY

A LITTLE, LATE

Enid Stubin

Y ou're not supposed to be reading that – it's *personal*.' He snatched away the lab report, but I'd already read it upside down and saw how bad things were. Eleven tickets to the Metropolitan Opera season would have to be parceled out. But the game was to ignore the words (*adenocarcinoma, metastatic*) and make the apartment habitable for a dying man. The chaos and extravagant squalor of my cousin Lester's apartment, a place I'd never seen before in our decade of companionship and rollicking fun, posed a challenge: a hallway heaped high with broken picture frames, lame shopping carts, wonky umbrellas; glamorous china of the 1970s entombed in dusty cartons lining the living room with its five television sets, only one of which worked thanks to an elaborate counterbalance of pliers and crumpled aluminium foil; cut crystal goblets thickly sifted with roach droppings and perched precariously on sticky kitchen surfaces; blackout window treatments fashioned of plastic trash bags, bamboo dowels, and wooden clothespins. Our Lester was a cheerful vampire, up all night cooking elaborate meals and watching public television, mostly British period dramas and Sherlock Holmes, sleeping through the daylight hours until he rose at 4:00 to breakfast on hot Wheatena and to take his 'tubbing' in the sarcophagus-sized bath.

But after the PET scan, the doctor sent an ambulance, and his sister Shirley and I convened, on Lester's birthday, in the hospital emergency room. After surgery, he would not be going home. So home would have to be reimagined and strict secrecy maintained (Lester's command. 'I don't want people to feel sad when they think of me'). One of the world's ardent eaters, Lester now refused food as well as a rental television. But when Peter arrived with a Zabar's croissant, savoury or sweet, Lester agreed to consume half. In on the conspiracy, Larry called every other day and over the phone provided a private piano recital, favoring Mozart's early sonatas, Scarlatti's peppier suites, and Chopin's mazurkas. (The days in between, Larry confided, he practiced.) I lugged *The Complete Sherlock Holmes* to a series of surprisingly large, sunlit hospital rooms in Borough Park, Brooklyn. Nurtured on Basil Rathbone movies and Granada television productions (Lester treasured a copy of *The Reader* No. 26, with its essay by Edward Hardwicke, as a link between two generations of Holmesiana), he saw no reason to read ('Why would I?' he asked, genuinely puzzled) but agreed to be read to.

We began with some of his favorites, but Lester was disappointed by 'The Adventure of the Twisted Lip', a story with particular resonance for him, as its protagonist lived a double life busking for spare change on the streets of London and amassing a tidy amount. But it didn't 'read' well. I scored a hit with 'The Red-Headed League', which called for several levels of Cockney characterization and sound effects managed with a sturdy umbrella. 'A Scandal in Bohemia' also required dialect. Unfortunately, my King of Bohemia sounded like Boris Badenov until, halfway through, I managed some convincing Hapsburg bluster to balance what I could replicate of Jeremy Brett's quicksilver shifts in tone. For Lester 'A Scandal in Bohemia' was *the* story.

In the step-down unit, with its gorgeous views of New York Harbor (and where I was busted by a nurse in the patients' toilet, having an unauthorized pee), I tried out *A Christmas Carol*, but Lester was skeptical that such a slim paperback could yield all the Cruikshank crabbiness of Reginald Owen, the roast beef and neurosis of Alastair Sims' Scrooge. We rationed ourselves to a stave a day, to maintain suspense and because I feared wearying him. But he marveled at the wealth of detail and, a fanatic of the visual, saw what narrative could do, exulting, 'Enid, the language, the *language*!'

Then the storm hit. I was on the phone with Lester when a Con Edison transformer awash in seawater exploded quite spectacularly on Fourteenth Street, and the lights south of Thirty-ninth Street went out. Luddite that I am, I had one of the only landlines in the building and curly-corded access to areas where cellular reception was cut off. The trains and buses weren't running, so travel to Brooklyn was impossible for five days. Unable to visit Lester, I was heartened by the arrival of The London Eye, newly posted in the city for a month and ensconced in an Upper East Side flat that looked like a bachelor pad from a 1960s Tony Curtis movie. Over a cup of Earl Grey, I asked her what I should read to Lester. *Bleak House*, of course. Lester balked at the Norton Critical Edition, the size and weight of a cinder block, that I carried to his room in the nursing home in Bensonhurst. He expected good production values, adored Gillian Anderson, and couldn't imagine anyone approaching her wounded froideur as Lady Dedlock. But let's face it, he was a captive audience. His room, a little shabby and sad, was nonetheless luxurious when compared to the wreck of the apartment I despaired of making livable, with a free phone and a little television where Lester could watch Eyewitness News and *Inspector Lewis*. His big sister Shirley, in cheerful attendance virtually every day, sat at one side of the bed, knitting woolen helmet liners for soldiers and reminiscing over the childhood shenanigans that Lester termed 'bits', while I took the other side and tried to summon up the rainy drear of Chesney Wold. Lester savored the descriptions and dialogue, conducting each phrase with a lilting gesture of his hand. It was music to him.

Two of Lester's nurses hung on his spirited tales of the opera. They'd never been. That was all Lester needed to hear: Peter organised two tickets to *Aida*, and the yelps of delight as Rebecca and Sugar hurled themselves onto Lester's bed evoked Christmas morning at Grandpa's. Another nurse, Rachele, tricked Lester into revealing his true first name, which he hated: she was planning to name her first son after him.

Lester had retired early from the workaday world; a gifted artisan, he didn't like the change of management, the shift in the shop, and so quit. '*Ee*nid, I feel *exactly* the way I felt at nine years old. And then I look in the mirror and I see an old man that I have to support and take care of.' My friends were crazy about him: he welcomed guests on New Year's Eve with a glass of Champagne and created the admixture of liberty and fun that as children we hope adulthood will yield but rarely does.

Conversation had never been labored between us and wasn't even now, when, despite the kindness and tact of his nurses, pain and indignity bruised each day, but the world outside was retreating. I needn't have worried about days of treatment and fees, despite Lester's wistful sense of longitudinal time. '*Ee*nid, I don't want to leave you and Shirley and all our wonderful friends. But six months, a year… it's so *long*.' That estimate reflected the oncologist's reckoning had Lester agreed to chemo; it now seemed unlikely – although it might have allowed us to read *Great Expectations* and *Little Dorrit*. As it was, we made it to 'Deportment' in *Bleak House*. Lester was moved to a hospice and slept most of the day, even when I arrived ready to give Esther Summerson a little mettle and describe Charles Dance's press during the furor over *The Jewel in the Crown* as 'the thinking girl's crumpet'.

The last night I saw him, he seemed to retreat when I wished, as always, to hang out, to tell one more story. But our cousin Arlen, who'd been allowed only in the last week to know how sick he was and who'd grown up with a gallant, dashing Lester, knew him well. She thought he was trying to tell me something. I leaned down and heard his murmured 'Enough.' When the phone rang at three in the morning, I knew it was Shirley with the news. In the cab on the way to Brooklyn, she and Arlen and I huddled, released from care, determined to do our best for him. Behind the curtain that had been drawn around the bed, there was no Lester left. I took the books from the bedside.

I need to read them again.

YOUR REGULARS

ASK THE READER

Brian Nellist

Q Curiosity has recently made me look back at the Border Ballads that I last read in the lower forms of my secondary school, over fifty years ago. Recollected pleasure was now replaced by boredom. They are full of set phrases and above all repetition, the unmistakeable signs of limited imagination and formalised vocabulary. Surely they belong with other delights we grow out of – in effect nursery rhymes for eleven-year-olds?

A Few children first meet nursery rhymes through the printed page. They hear them from the mouths of adults and, here's hoping they still do, they gain thereby a feeling for rhythmic language and discover that words don't always need a rational equivalent, 'Hickory, dickory, dock' or even 'Hey nonny no'. They are remnants of that oral tradition of poetry which lies behind, though, not simply in Homer and *Beowulf* and the *Chanson de Roland*, first cousins to modern performance poetry and rap. Like the ballads and refrains in our older songs, they appeal to communal memory. You are objecting I think to that sense of the 'again' in literature. But 'again' is a mysterious not a worn-out language feature. 'No man steps twice into the same river' said Heraclitus because the water always changes as does the significance of words. 'I am sick, I must die / Lord have mercy on us' ends each stanza of Nashe's poem 'Adieu, farewell earth's bliss'. Of course the eye takes it in at a glance of the printed page but hearing it one has first to recognise the repetition, then realise that the stanzas compose a litany and increasingly see how the value of it is subtly altered by the context of the proceeding lines. It appeals not primarily to the analytical mind but to the feelings aroused by the sense of inevitability. 'Widdecombe Fair' is a song about a local calamity but the refrain 'Old Uncle Tom Cobleigh and all' restores a sense of communal well-being.

Among Wordsworth's *Lyrical Ballads* there is an interesting note on his poem 'The Thorn' in which he defends the use of repetition. He reminds the reader that 'virtual tautology is much oftener produced by using different words when the meaning is exactly the same' and goes on to argue, less contentiously maybe, that to keep using the same words may signal 'a craving in the mind' to express feelings that are unutterable; 'as long as it is unsatisfied the speaker will cling to the same words'. Repetition becomes the signifier of inarticulate passion. Martha Ray in the poem is a village girl abandoned by her lover who loses her reason and seeks shelter on a hill-top to deliver her child away from gossip and unfriendly eyes. But what actually happened up there the speaker, a stranger to the district, wonders:

> **No more I know, I wish I did**
> **And I would tell it all to you;**
> **There's none that ever knew:**
> **And if a child was born or no**
> **There's no one that could ever tell;**
> **And if 'twas born alive or dead**
> **There's no one knows as I have said.**

The crucial repetition is 'know' so that the speaker, well-intentioned though he is, misses the crucial point and seems close to one of the scandal-mongers in the settlement. Was the baby still-born, did it die of exposure, did Martha kill it as so many girls in her condition did? 'Tell' is another repetition, as though her sufferings become simply an item in local gossip. But behind his blundering inarticulacy there lies a deeper responsiveness for which he can find no words;

> **And she is known to every star,**
> **And every wind that blows.**

What a different effect of the conjunction 'and' and what an accepting 'know' against the forensic 'know' in the other lines. Judgement is irrelevant in the face of pity.

Words come circling back, as in the Border Ballads; 'I wish I were where Helen lies / On fair Kirconnell Lee', for example. You must find the Bible difficult reading if you dislike repetition. Modernist literature with its concern for the involuntary processes of the mind often reiterates phrases as in Lawrence or Eliot or Virginia Woolf, whose work is oral rather than silent. Philip Davis recently got me to read a novel by Kirsty Gunn, *The Big Music* (2012), an account of a Highland piping family. The title translates the Gaelic *piobaireachd*, the masterpiece of pipe music which in its different sections can become a personal history of its composer. The central figure, an aging father on the edge of dementia, has been increasingly absorbed by the creation of one piece to measure against his own father's work:

playing his father's big music, the Big Music, again and playing it again and again. Why bother then, you might say, about anything else? What need for anyone? Any conversation, any thought for another? When there was this at the centre of it, music. There need be nothing else. No friends, no wife, no child.

Each 'again' has a different and intensifying value as it does for a phrase in a musical performance (or the reading aloud of a novel one might add). The multiplying 'any's remind us of the terrible price paid by the devotion to a craft (or any absolute devotion, I suppose), and they chillingly lead up to 'anyone' or 'another', where 'otherness' has a human face being rejected. 'Any' that inclusive word ends in the final exclusions of 'No friends, no wife, no child'. Rejection here is not a simple point hammered home but a terrible testing on the feelings of an approach to the absolute zero without any intrusive comment by the bewigged and ermined figure of the reason sitting in the high court of the mind. Feel the drama of a man cutting away all his connections to the earth and recognise that it's the repetitions that make you experience it.

Minted, Practical Poetry for Life, edited by Brian Nellist

To buy:
Please send a cheque for
£6 to The Reader
Organisation:

The Reader Organisation (Minted), The Friary Centre,
Bute Street, Liverpool, L5 3LA
See www.thereader.org.uk for more details

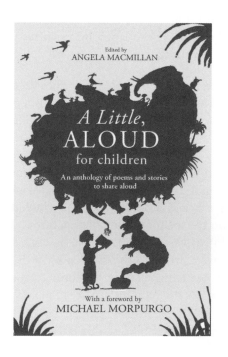

Financial Times
Book of the Year
for Children

'An absolutely
impeccable
anthology'

£9.99 RRP

Or £5.99 (+ p&p)
from www.thereader.org.uk

YOUR RECOMMENDATIONS

BOOKS ABOUT...

INTENSITY

Angela Macmillan

Strictly speaking these books are not so much about intensity as intense in themselves. They are novels that use up your whole attention; reading them is like entering a separate space of time in which a part of you remains, even when you have put down the book. Perhaps the intensity comes from the relationship between author and reader, as if the writing is so deeply imagined that the reader cannot fail to be affected.

Denis Johnson, *Train Dreams* (2012)
Granta; ISBN-13: 978-1847086617

This short, hugely concentrated novel, tells of a railroad labourer, Robert Grainier whose story – tracking a sweep of American Frontier history – begins in the 1880s when as an orphan he is sent by train to live with cousins in Idaho, his destination pinned to his chest on the back of a store receipt, and ends in the 1950s outside a train carrying Elvis Presley. Grainier is an ordinary, uneducated man whose life is overwhelmed by strangeness and tragedy. As he becomes more and more solitary, so the surface of reality cracks open into the dream-like or visionary lying so closely beneath. The book is full of juxtapositions, the epic with the small, the fantastic with the ordinary, the natural with the mechanical. It is unsettling and compelling.

Wallace Stegner, *Crossing to Safety* **(1987)**
Penguin Modern Classics; ISBN-13: 978-0141188010

Stegner's final book is the story of a lifelong friendship between two couples in 1930's Wisconsin where Larry and Sally Morgan first meet Sid and Charity Lang, the proverbial golden couple. The men are junior academics in the English department at Madison University and the wives are both pregnant. Careers, children and life happen. There is nothing showy or sensational here: 'How do you make a book that anyone will read out of lives as quiet as these?' is one of the questions of the novel. If you read this intelligent, compassionate, wise novel you will find out. One of the best books I have read recently.

Honoré de Balzac, *Eugénie Grandet* **(1833)**
Vintage Classics; ISBN-13: 978-0099560869

'To arrive fully at the truth', said Balzac, 'writers use whatever literary device seems capable of giving the greatest intensity of life to their characters'. Like Dickens, Balzac's characters were as real to him as if they lived and breathed beside him. Monsieur Grandet is obsessed with money – having and holding on to it. His wife and daughter are victims of his extreme miserliness and live lives of strict hardship. Into this dull, mean house comes the exquisitely flamboyant Charles, nephew to Grandet, with whom Eugénie falls deeply in love. Eugénie's moving story is told with humanity and delicacy.

Georgina Harding, *The Painter of Silence* **(2012)**
Bloomsbury; ISBN-13: 978-1408830420

The place is Romania, the timespan of the novel takes us from the 1930s to the 1950s, from feudalism to communism. The central figure, Augustin, is born deaf and never learns speech but he does have an acute visual memory and the talent to draw what he sees and remembers. As the son of a servant on a wealthy estate he grows up with Safta, daughter of the house. The war changes everything and parts them. Augustin's struggle to make sense of the world is at the heart of this tender, thoughtful book and leads to big questions about language, memory, silence, home and identity. Georgina Harding is one of our best current writers and deserves a lot more attention and readers

Chad Harbach, *The Art of Fielding* **(2012)**
Fourth Estate ISBN-13: 978-0007374458

Henry Skrimshander lives for baseball. It is his life. What happens when a life is denied its purpose is the subject of the book. A huge success in USA; publishers fought over the UK paperback rights but I think this novel has not quite fulfilled expectations here. The British have yet to fall in love with baseball. I know nothing about the sport, yet this did not spoil my enjoyment for it is about so much more than baseball as *Moby Dick*, the book that exists behind this one, is about much more than whales. Essentially it is an old-fashioned (in the best way) rite of passage novel and although it would have benefited from strict editing in the second half, it is definitely worth reading.

A LITTLE *MORE* ALOUD

ELIZABETH GASKELL
NORTH AND SOUTH

Selected by Angela Macmillan

Here, for reading aloud, is a taster of Mrs Gaskell's wonderful, Manchester-based novel. Margaret Hale, a southerner, newly settled in the northern industrial town of Milton has visited the home of the local mill owner, Mr Thornton, at the very moment when an angry mob of striking mill workers has marched on his house to protest at the bringing in of Irish workers to do their jobs. Thornton is awaiting the arrival of the military; meanwhile, the Irishmen are trapped in a room in the mill.

'Mr. Thornton,' said Margaret, shaking all over with her passion, 'go down this instant, if you are not a coward. Go down and face them like a man. Save these poor strangers, whom you have decoyed here. Speak to your workmen as if they were human beings. Speak to them kindly. Don't let the soldiers come in and cut down poor-creatures who are driven mad. I see one there who is. If you have any courage or noble quality in you, go out and speak to them, man to man.'

He turned and looked at her while she spoke. A dark cloud came over his face while he listened. He set his teeth as he heard her words.

'I will go. Perhaps I may ask you to accompany me downstairs, and bar the door behind me; my mother and sister will need that protection.'

'Oh! Mr. Thornton! I do not know – I may be wrong – only –'

But he was gone; he was downstairs in the hall; he had unbarred the front door; all she could do, was to follow him quickly, and fasten it behind him, and clamber up the stairs again with a sick heart and a dizzy head. Again she took her place by the farthest window. He was on the steps below; she saw that by the direction of a thousand angry eyes; but she could neither see nor hear any-thing save the savage satisfaction of the rolling angry murmur. She threw the window wide open. Many in the crowd were mere boys; cruel and thoughtless, – cruel because they were thoughtless; some were men, gaunt as wolves, and mad for prey. She knew how it was; they were like Boucher, with starving children at home – relying on ultimate success in their efforts to get higher wages, and enraged beyond measure at discovering that Irishmen were to be brought in to rob their little ones of bread. Margaret knew it all; she read it in Boucher's face, forlornly desperate and livid with rage. If Mr. Thornton would but say something to them – let them hear his voice only – it seemed as if it would be better than this wild beating and raging against the stony silence that vouchsafed them no word, even of anger or reproach. But perhaps he was speaking now; there was a momentary hush of their noise, inarticulate as that of a troop of animals. She tore her bonnet off; and bent forwards to hear. She could only see; for if Mr. Thornton had indeed made the attempt to speak, the momentary instinct to listen to him was past and gone, and the people were raging worse than ever. He stood with his arms folded; still as a statue; his face pale with repressed excitement. They were trying to intimidate him – to make him flinch; each was urging the other on to some immediate act of personal violence. Margaret felt intuitively, that in an instant all would be uproar; the first touch would cause an explosion, in which, among such hundreds of infuriated men and reckless boys, even Mr. Thornton's life would be unsafe, – that in another instant the stormy passions would have passed their bounds, and swept away all barriers of reason, or apprehension of consequence. Even while she looked, she saw lads in the back-ground stooping to take off their heavy wooden clogs – the readiest missile they could find; she saw it was the spark to the gunpowder, and, with a cry, which no one heard, she rushed out of the room, down stairs, – she had lifted the great iron bar of the door with an imperious force – had thrown the door open wide – and was there, in face of that angry sea of men, her eyes smiting them with flaming arrows of reproach. The clogs were arrested in the hands that held them – the countenances, so fell not a moment before, now looked irresolute, and as if asking what this meant. For she stood between them and their enemy. She could not speak, but held out her arms towards them till she could recover breath.

'Oh, do not use violence! He is one man, and you are many; but her words died away, for there was no tone in her voice; it was but a hoarse whisper. Mr. Thornton stood a little on one side; he had moved away from behind her, as if jealous of anything that should come between him and danger.

'Go!' said she, once more (and now her voice was like a cry). 'The soldiers are sent for – are coming. Go peaceably. Go away. You shall have relief from your complaints, whatever they are.'

'Shall them Irish blackguards be packed back again?' asked one from out the crowd, with fierce threatening in his voice.

'Never, for your bidding!' exclaimed Mr. Thornton. And instantly the storm broke. The hootings rose and filled the air, – but Margaret did not hear them. Her eye was on the group of lads who had armed themselves with their clogs some time before. She saw their gesture – she knew its meaning, – she read their aim. Another moment, and Mr. Thornton might be smitten down, – he whom she had urged and goaded to come to this perilous place. She only thought how she could save him. She threw her arms around him; she made her body into a shield from the fierce people beyond. Still, with his arms folded, he shook her off.

'Go away,' said he, in his deep voice. 'This is no place for you.'

BUCK'S QUIZ

IT'S GRIM UP NORTH

Angela Macmillan

1. 'T'maister nobbut just buried and Sabbath not o'ered und t'sound o' t' gospel still i yer lugs and ye darr be laiking!' Who is speaking?

2. 'All I'm out for is a good time – all the rest is propaganda.' Who is this working class hero?

3. 'Whats that?' 'That's the moor. Does tha like it?' 'No, I hate it'. 'That's because tha'rt not used to it. Tha thinks it's is too big and bare now. But tha' will like it.' Who are the two speakers?

4. 'Dang the wall-eyed bay, he's gone mad wi glory I think, cause t' coorch is over.' Who lends a hand when the coach for Yorkshire turns over?

5. Who lives in the fictional Yorkshire town of Stradhoughton?

6. How does Frank Machin earn a living in Wakefield?

7. 'I wish I could tell you how lonely I am. How cold and harsh it is here. Everywhere there is conflict, unkindness. I think God has forsaken this place.' Who says this after having to leave her tranquil rural home in the south of England?

8. 'He told, that to these waters he had come / To gather leeches being old and poor: / Employment hazardous and wearisome! / And he had many hardships to endure'. What is the poem's title?

9. '"The Bottoms" succeeded to "Hell Row". Hell Row was a block of thatched, bulging cottages that stood by the brookside on Greenhill Lane. There lived the colliers who worked in the little gin-pits two fields away.' The opening words to which novel?

10. Which childhood memoir ends: 'Tha' leaving Lancashire,' my friend said, as he slammed in the gear. 'Cheshire's at top of 'ill.' 'Good-bye Lancashire,' I said, a frog in my throat.'

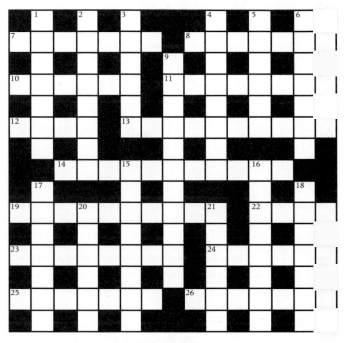

ACROSS

7. Dissenting group in docudrama (7)
***8.** See 17 down
10 and 24. After dark we hear him wandering in search of adventure (6, 6)
11. Former palmer turns into paragon (8)
***12 and 23.** She is introduced in one station and leaves us in another (4, 8)
***13.** T. S. Eliot confused about the smallest room. Another writer? (3, 7)
***14.** Novel article with a new red cap circulating (3, 3, 5)
19. Local bears turn on Spanish gentleman (10)
22. Notice bruise (4)
***23.** See 12 across
24. See 10 across
25. This is held to be a call for silence in Edinburgh (7)
26. Notices comments (7)

DOWN

1. Sunrise can make a large number blind (7)
2. Blessed marks single disgrace (8)
3. Deadly person (6)
4. Bird sanctuary disturbed by Coriolanus? (8)
5. Southern poets round on Marie who wanted to limit issues (6)
6. A Latin road to the top for high flyer (7)
9. Additional action needed to reach a conclusion (6, 5)
15. This is fine if a bit one-sided (3, 5)
16. Country's geological period (8)
***17 and 8 across.** Heroine of 14 who escapes 12's fate despite trying (7, 7)
***18.** Old queen on TV channel points to lover of 12 across (7)
20. Teresa led astray on these high trails (6)
21. Views tantrums (6)

*Clues with an asterisk have a common theme

PRIZES

The winner of the Crossword (plucked in time-honoured tradition from a hat) will receive a book prize courtesy of Vintage Classics, and the same to the winner of the fiendishly difficult Buck's Quiz.

Congratulations to Alison Linklater of Penicuik, Midlothian, who won both Buck's Quiz and the Crossword prizes.

Please send your solutions (marked Cassandra Crossword or Buck's Quiz) to The Reader Organisation, The Friary Centre, Bute Street, Liverpool, L5 3LA. The deadline for answers is 5 July, 2013.

ANSWERS

CASSANDRA CROSSWORD NO. 41

Across
1. Anthony 5. Obadiah 9. Inwit 10. The Warden 11. Barchester 12. Scum 14. Adventitious 18. Dermabrasion 21. Milk 22. China girls 25. Two button 26. Ennui 27. Reekier 28. Harding

Down
1. Akimbo 2. Towers 3. Octahedral 4. Yetis 5. Omelettes 6. Alas 7. Inductor 8. Hindmost 13. Strong beer 15. Earthstar 16. Odometer 17. Trollope 19. Brunei 20. Asking 23. Ninth 24. Puri

BUCK'S QUIZ NO. 48

1. Sherlock Holmes 2. Hercule Poirot 3. Philip Marlowe 4. Father Brown 5. John Rebus 6. Sam Spade 7. Nancy Drew 8. Lord Peter Wimsey 9. Kurt Wallander 10. Jules Maigret

FICTION

BUDDHA OF THE ULTIMATE REALITY

Sian Davis

On his thirtieth birthday, Thomas awoke with an urgent sense that something was slipping though his fingers. He sat up in bed trying to work out what. Though his short dark curls were already peppered with white, he was still an obviously young man, whose defining moments were yet to come. It weighed heavily on him.

Light shone onto the ceiling, reflected from passing cars on the street below, shimmers of stained glass red, blue, silver. The room was a kind of loose pinhole camera created by the darkened space within it and the tiny sliver of light at the top of the curtains. Thomas found himself thinking about Renaissance paintings, and how someone less cynical might have had an epiphany at that moment; yes, he thought, you wake up in a state of existential despair and as if by magic, the solution presents itself to you – the consolations of art and religion.

As he lay listening to the morning street sounds outside his window he could feel a spring tightening in his stomach. He needed a cigarette. On the table next to his bed one remained in a crushed packet. Thomas lit it and lay on his back, savouring the smoke. Then he got up, showered and dressed, and made coffee. He let in next door's cat, a sleek grey Burmese who as usual was sitting waiting at the back door, tail curled neatly around her legs with a calm air of entitlement. Finding a tin of sardines in someone else's cupboard he appropriated them and speared one out for the cat, smiling at the appreciative noises she made as she licked her oily muzzle afterwards. He'd never liked cats before, but this one would sit next to him companionably when he attempted to get on with his work, purring and butting her head against his writing hand.

I have to start work now, he thought, and get going before the bad feelings get me. He cast a glance over at his desk, piled high with a mess of books, papers and the files containing his incomplete thesis. It was no use; the coffee had made his pulse race unpleasantly. The spring began tightening again. On impulse, he turned from the cluttered desk and grabbed his jacket. As he opened the front door, the cat shot out and nimbly jumped up onto the wall where it settled down to watch him as he locked the door and made his way across the street in the direction of the meadows.

All around him students were going about their daily business, whizzing past on cycles or carrying cups of takeaway coffee towards the lecture halls. He had difficulty navigating through them. Every time he passed someone on the narrow pavement he veered slightly into them, or stopped and tried to guess which side they would pass on, incurring several irritated glances. The blood rose to his cheeks. He looked carefully left and right but somehow stepped immediately into the path of a cyclist who swerved to avoid him, angrily hissing something that Thomas didn't quite catch. Crossing over the road he suddenly felt the sky yawning open above him, and his face began to freeze into a mask of panic. He felt his mouth beginning to open into a gape of horror. Ahead of him was the museum forecourt, fortuitously empty of people at this time of the morning. He stumbled through the gates to the benches at the side of the courtyard and sat down heavily, feeling inside his coat pocket for a cigarette.

He let the cigarette smoke out slowly, regulating his breathing and watching the curls of smoke hang. As the panic subsided, he heard a high-pitched melodious twittering above him. Up in the branches of the yew that spread over the edge of the courtyard, he saw a tiny bird hopping from one branch to the next, buff green and smaller than a wren, with a tiny fiery gold stripe on its head. Thomas kept absolutely still, watching the jewel-like creature as it inched from twig to twig, closer to him. It held its head to one side as it regarded Thomas, its whole body nerve-bound and ready to flutter away at the slightest threat. A blackbird scooted noisily down into the courtyard to peck at a discarded apple by the bin and when Thomas looked up again, the tiny bird had gone.

In the museum there were two pictures that Thomas always went to see: a simple still life by Henri Fantin-Latour of a white bone china cup and saucer against a dark chocolate background, and a sketchy oil painting by Degas of two women in a café. Not the most illustrious paintings, they radiated a sense of extraordinary reality. The white cup and saucer seemed to Thomas to be exactly what a cup and saucer should be, as if this was the original cup and saucer on which all others were modelled. With the Degas, he sensed the difficulty of the conversation between the two women, oblivious to their café surroundings. One listened, concerned, while the other was hesitantly telling her secret, a smudgy impressionistic orange on the table between them. Looking at that painting he always half expected them to look up and frown at him for eavesdropping.

Feeling more anchored now, he wandered through the Islamic pottery section until he reached the special exhibition space in the central hall. Here, a visiting display from the British Museum was arranged: a collection of eastern art. A shaven-headed old woman with saffron and wine-coloured robes beneath her raincoat was standing stock still in front of one the statues. Of all the statues in the display, this one certainly drew the eye: a Buddha figure, the dark volcanic rock from which it was carved appearing to sparkle and glisten as if it was newly hewn. The Buddha was frozen mid leap, its leg raised up as if it was going to jump. Thomas found himself drawn towards it. It seemed to fix him with a hawk-like penetrating gaze.

'You feel that it's alive, but just very, very still, don't you?' the old woman said, standing next to him conspiratorially, her eyes bright and birdlike.

'It reminds me of those clay animations of Greek myths and legends in films from the sixties and seventies,' replied Thomas. 'It's about to lean over, hop off the plinth, and get me.'

'You find it frightening?' asked the woman.

'Not frightening. Not threatening.' Thomas searched for the words. 'Just very alive. More alive than me, maybe.'

The woman smiled, giving a little nod of her head as she turned back to the statue. Thomas also remained standing there, aware of the sunlight filtering through the high windows. A feeling of space, the exact opposite of the crowded, jostling feeling of outside, began to unfold in him. As he stood looking at the statue he was flooded with a sudden sense of recognition.

Thomas felt then as he sometimes did on waking from a dream, that some great secret had been revealed to him, so startlingly obvious that he was amazed that he hadn't realised it before. But just as on those occasions, as soon as he made the realisation, it began to ebb away. He stood in the hall of figures looking at the sparkling statue whose half smile now seemed slightly mocking. He leant in to look at the label on the plinth. It read:

'Buddha of the Ultimate Reality. Borobudur, West Java. 9th Century.'

Well of course, thought Thomas.

The old woman was looking at him quizzically.

'Forgive me, but you seem to be caught between a rock and a hard place,' she said, gesturing towards the statue. With an earnest incline of the head, she willed Thomas to smile at her little joke.

'Tea,' she prescribed. 'It calms you when you are over stimulated, and cheers you when you are low. Won't you join me?' she asked, and moved her arm gently in the direction of the museum café.

His throat tightened around a lump, and Thomas nodded silently and followed her over to the empty café where they sat beneath the glass-vaulted roof of the museum's modern extension. A young woman served them a pot of tea and went back to cleaning the coffee machine behind the counter. The old woman sipped her tea. She did not speak; she waited.

Blinking back a prickle of tears, Thomas clutched his cup of tea, enjoying the half pain half pleasure sensation of the heat of the white china cup in his hands. Then, in faltering tones, glancing over at the girl behind the counter to ensure she wasn't listening, he told the woman of his life gone wrong. As he related the false turns he'd taken, the near derailment of his Ph.D and his feeling of losing touch with reality, he finally felt the spring in his stomach begin to unwind.

The old woman calmly considered what he had said. She looked at him shrewdly.

'So, you have been though some testing times and have come out the other side without losing everything. With some hard work you can finish your studies on time, and you just feel that you should pull yourself up by your bootstraps. Is that it?'

'It feels more hopeless than that.' At that moment Thomas did not feel quite so hopeless anymore.

'Here's a question' said the old woman, 'When you were looking at that statue, did you feel hopeless then?'

'No,' said Thomas 'I felt absolved somehow.'

'And nothing actually changed, am I right? For a moment, you forgot your unhappiness.'

Thomas nodded.

'Perhaps you could change the way you think about things more often?' she continued. 'Like flexing a muscle you don't use very often. Start small, exercise frequently.'

'What should I do?' asked Thomas.

But the old woman just smiled at him and drained her cup.

'I hope you feel better,' she said, as she got up to leave the table, 'I enjoyed talking with you.'

'Thank you for the tea,' said Thomas.

He sat there for a while. He had expected the woman to make some kind of religious overture to him, and had been sceptically waiting for it, but it never came. The woman had simply recognised his distress and tried to help him. For the first time in a while Thomas felt light in his skin. The tension in his stomach was gone.

As he left the museum he passed through the gift shop near the exit, and was just about to go out through the revolving door when someone spoke behind him.

'Excuse me, sir?' It was the gift shop attendant.

'Yes?'

'The woman that just left asked me to give you this,' she said. She handed him a paper gift shop bag with some kind of card inside.

'Really?' said Thomas.

'Yes, the nun. She left it for you just now.'

Thomas took the bag and thanked her. He put it in his pocket and left the museum. The street was not so busy now, and he walked along the narrow pavement without passing anyone. He wandered down to the meadows, stopping when he came to the river. He took the paper bag from his pocket. Inside was a postcard from the museum shop. On it, in a clear hand, read the message:

'There are many realities, but only one moment. Try it.'

Thomas turned the postcard over. It was the little white cup and saucer on the dark chocolate background. Still life, he thought to himself.

CONTRIBUTORS

Connie Bensley was born in south-west London, and has always lived there, apart from wartime evacuation. Until her retirement she worked as a secretary to doctors and to an M.P. and as a medical copywriter. Her latest book from Bloodaxe is *Finding a Leg to Stand On: New & Selected Poems* (2012).

David Constantine's most recent story collection is *Tea at the Midland* (Comma 2012). His latest poetry collection *Nine Fathoms Deep* is published by Bloodaxe. With his wife Helen he edits *Modern Poetry in Translation*.

Frank Cottrell Boyce is an award winning novelist and screen writer. He was the writer for the 2012 Summer Olympics opening ceremony. His most recent books are sequels to Ian Fleming's *Chitty Chitty Bang Bang*.

Charles Darby-Villis is RISE (Reading in Secure Environments) co-ordinator & Reader-in-Residence, HMP Low Newton, Durham.

Sian Davis lives in Cambridge and is currently studying for a degree in English Literature with the Open University.

Casi Dylan is Literary Learning Manager at The Reader Organisation, where she has worked since 2008. Born in Cwmystwyth, Ceredigion, she now lives in Glasgow although her work has taken her all over the UK as well as Denmark and Australia.

Priscilla Gilman is a former assistant professor of English literature at both Yale University and Vassar College. *The Anti-Romantic Child* was a Best Book of 2011 for both the Leonard Lopate Show and the *Chicago Tribune*, and was one of five nominees for a Books for a Better Life Award for Best First Book.

Phillip Jupitus is a writer, broadcaster and performer from Essex who likes the poetry of Ian Dury, baseball and 1960s Jamaican Ska.

Ian McMillan was born in 1956 and has been a freelance writer/performer/broadcaster since 1981. He presents *The Verb* on BBC Radio 3 every Friday night.

Alexis McNay is a Criminal Justice Project Worker for The Reader Organisation.

Blake Morrison is a poet and novelist. His memoir, *And When Did You Last See Your Father?* won the J.R. Ackerly Prize for Autobiography. Non-fiction books include *As If* (1997), about the James Bulger case. His novel *The Last Weekend* was recently dramatised for television. *A Discoverie of Witches,* containing a sequence of poems about the Pendle Witch trials, appeared last year.

Andrew Motion is a poet, novelist, and biographer. Poet Laureate (1999–2009); founder of Poetry Archive (www.poetryarchive.org); President of the Campaign to Protect Rural England. His most recent collection is *The Customs House* (Faber and Faber). His sequel to *Treasure Island*, *Silver:Return to Treasure Island* is published by Vintage 2013.

Les Murray is Australia's leading poet. He has won many literary awards, including the Grace Leven Prize (1980 and 1990), the Petrarch Prize (1995), and the prestigious TS Eliot Award (1996). In 1999 he was awarded the Queens Gold Medal for Poetry on the recommendation of Ted Hughes.

Anthony Rudolf's book of poems *Zigzag* (Carcanet/Northern House) was published in 2010. A short memoir about his childhood autograph album *A Vanished Hand* was published by Shearsman this year. He is working on new essays about Primo Levi and George Oppen.

Michael Stewart's novel *King Crow* is the winner of the *Guardian*'s Not The Booker Award. He writes plays for BBC radio and for theatre. His short fiction has been published widely. For more information please visit his website: www.michael-stewart.org.uk

Enid Stubin is Assistant Professor of English at Kingsborough Community College of the City University of New York and Adjunct Professor of Humanities at NY University's School of Continuing and Professional Studies.

Rowan Williams grew up in South Wales and studied Theology in Cambridge, later doing research in Oxford on Russian religious thought. After an eventful period as Archbishop of Canterbury, he is now back in Cambridge as Master of Magdalene College, hoping to find more time for reading and writing. He has published several collections of poetry'

Distribution Information

Trade orders Contact Mark Chilver, Magazine Department, Central Books

email: mark@centralbooks.com
web: www.centralbooks.com
tel: 0845 458 9925   fax: 0845 458 9912
Central Books, 99 Wallis Road, London, E9 5LN

All other queries regarding trade orders or institutional subscriptions
Contact The Reader Office

email: magazine@thereader.org.uk
tel: 0151 207 7207

SUBSCRIBE

Just £18 per year with Direct Debit

Either print off an order form from our website (www.
thereader.org.uk), call us on 0151 207 7207 or email
(magazine@thereader.org.uk) and we will send you a form
in the post.

Cost by Cheque or PayPal:

UK   4 issues   £24.00   (including p&p)
Abroad   4 issues   £36.00   (including p&p)

Please make cheques payable to The Reader Organisation
and post to: The Reader Organisation, FREEPOST RSSL-
UHCB-EKKE, The Friary Centre, Bute Street, Liverpool,
L5 3LA.

Don't forget to include your name and address, and the
issue number with which you would like your subscrip-
tion to begin.

Overseas readers: your cheapest method is by PayPal via
our website: www.thereader.org.uk.

Please direct email enquiries to:
subscriptions@thereader.org.uk

the reader